EARTHQUAKE

ROBERT L. IACOPI

COUNTRY

Publishers: Fred W. Fisher
                     Howard W. Fisher

Editor: Fred W. Fisher
Editorial Assistant: Alison Fisher

Book Design: Josh Young
Cover Design: Josh Young

Production Manager: Deanie Wood
Book Production: Randy Schultz

Cover photograph: Larry Ulrich Photography
                     *Padres shooting stars and blue oaks, with the Gabilan mountain range in the
                     background. Photo taken in Pinnacles National Moument in San Benito County.*

**Library of Congress
Cataloging-in-Publication Data**

Iacopi, Robert.
    Earthquake country / Robert L. Iacopi. — 4th ed.
      p.   cm.
    Includes index.
    ISBN 1-55561-086-2
    1. Earthquakes-California.   I. Title.
QE535.I2   1996
551.2′2′09794—dc20
                                              96-9516
                                                 CIP

Published by Fisher Books
4239 W. Ina Road, Suite 101
Tucson, AZ 85741
(520) 744-6110

Disclaimer: This book is meant to be instructional, to provide information to help you understand the nature of fault movements and earthquakes, and to prepare you for the next earthquake. The information is believed to be accurate at the time of publication. Fault descriptions and illustrations of are based on published geologic sources, but are show only the general path of faults and may be subject to error. Readers are urged to make inquiries at the organizations listed on page 140 to obtain the most current information on earthquake hazards and the best methods of minimizing damage.

   The book is definitely and deliberately California-biased. Descriptions of faults and earthquakes are as accurate as possible for California only. No attempt has been made to factor in differences related to other parts of the world.

   The author and publisher disclaim all liability in connection with use of this book.

Table of Contents

Acknowledgments

This book leans heavily on the research, publications, and personal consultations of dozens of seismologists and geologists. I gratefully acknowledge the original work done by the dedicated professionals—past and present—at the U. S. Geological Survey, the California Division of Mines and Geology, California Institute of Technology, the National Earthquake Information Center, the Humboldt State Earthquake Center, and other public agencies. Without their original research and willingness to share their knowledge, there would be no *EARTHQUAKE COUNTRY*.

Special thanks to Drs. Lori Dengler of the Humboldt State Earthquake Center; Robert Brown, retired geologist; and Lucile Jones of USGS in Pasadena for taking time to read the manuscript and help improve its content and style. Others deserving individual mention include Mike Moore, David Wald, Robert Wallace, Malcolm Johnston, Linda Curtis, William Bakun, Charles Real, Carole Prentice, James Dewey, Dave Gordon, William Ellsworth, Paul Reasenberg and Steven Day.

Earl Hart and Chris Wills of the California Division of Mines and Geology were especially helpful in locating photos and technical material.

Katherine Frohmberg of the University of California's Earthquake Engineering Research Center (EERC) Library went out of her way to be helpful on selection and duplication of photographs.

Karl V. Steinbrugge lent considerable time and effort to the first edition of *EARTHQUAKE COUNTRY*, and improved this second effort by making his library of photos available through the EERC Library.

John Alderson, geologist/tour guide in Woodland Hills, provided personal guidance to other faults in Southern California.

E.R. 'Sandy' Hay, Professor of Geology at DeAnza College, helped explain fault and earthquake complexities with his classroom lectures and demonstrations.

Ted Evans and Mark Zielinski patiently provided long-term support and advice on the proper selection and use of computer hardware and software.

Jim Lyons generously opened his library of historical newspapers to help illustrate early California earthquakes.

Finally, a special acknowledgment to Ian Nicholas Dunn, who inspired me to attempt this project in the first place.

Preface

EARTHQUAKE COUNTRY is a revision of a book of the same name that was first published in 1964. It has been completely updated to reflect the significant changes in geological and seismological thought over the last 30 years. The San Andreas fault still is in the same place, but everything else has changed. The amount of data available to scientists, and the ability to analyze it, has increased dramatically and brought about some significant new theories.

One of the most important changes in scientific thinking is an understanding of the major significance of what once were considered to be minor, dormant faults throughout the state. Still another change has come in the understanding—or lack of it—about the complex nature of fault movements. Each new quake provides more information and another indication of the classic problem: The more we learn, the less we know for certain. On the positive side is our increased knowledge about structural requirements necessary to minimize death tolls during major quakes. Also, we are much more aware that a great deal can be done to minimize our personal property losses during and after such events.

This is the first edition of EARTHQUAKE COUNTRY that does not include a Foreword by Charles F. Richter, who passed away in 1985. Dr. Richter was very supportive of this project and was anxious for all Californians to understand the earthquake risks they assume by living here. In a Foreword prepared for an edition of EARTHQUAKE COUNTRY published in the 1970's, Dr. Richter turned out to be prophetic when he wrote ". . .the reader will find much information here not only about (the San Andreas fault system), but others not directly connected. This wider perspective is wholesome, and in the public interest...no locality in California is exempt from earthquake risk."

Re-publication of EARTHQUAKE COUNTRY also allows me to acknowledge the special contributions of Dr. Clarence Allen, geology professor emeritus at Cal Tech in Pasadena. Dr. Allen played a primary role in the creation and long-term success of the first edition, and has continued his personal support of the book for more than 30 years. Both his eminently successful professional career and his unselfish contributions to the general knowledge of the people of California deserve special recognition.

ROBERT L. IACOPI

Dedication:

To Carole,

in celebration of

40 years of

togetherness.

California's International Reputation

Chapter 1

Balboa Avenue in Granada Hills had the most spectacular damage in the 1994 Northridge earthquake. A destructive fire was caused by breaks in water mains and natural gas lines. Observers reported gas fumes ignited when the driver of a stalled truck attempted to restart the engine. For more details on this earthquake, see page 116. Photo by K. E. Sieh.

Despite its great variety of natural wonders, California may be best known internationally for just one thing—earthquakes. California *is* Earthquake Country. Many reports on its rumblings and shakings have made indelible impressions throughout the world.

Though sometimes exaggerated, California's position in the seismic world is indeed significant. It is part of the circum-Pacific seismic belt known as the *Ring of Fire* that is responsible for about 80 percent of the world's earthquakes and much of its volcanic activity.

All sections of this belt are typified by violent geologic activity and California is no exception. It has the San Andreas fault—one of the longest and most active tectonic features in the world—plus hundreds of other active faults. It also includes two volcanoes: Mt. Lassen, which erupted most recently in 1914, and Mt. Shasta.

Other spots around the Pacific Basin, such as Japan and Alaska, have more earthquakes. But California finishes high in the standings with thousands of shocks every year—500 strong enough to be felt by a significant number of residents.

Not all major earthquakes in the contiguous United States occur in California. Three of the largest in the national records occurred at New Madrid, Missouri (actually a series of four shocks between December 1811 and February 1812, with magnitudes as high as M7.8), Charleston, South Carolina (M7.0 in 1886), and Hegben Lake, Montana (M7.3 in 1959). But these were unusual events; California is the clear winner in frequency.

As long as there have been historians in California, there have been earthquake descriptions. As the Spanish exploration party led by Captain Gaspar de Portola walked from San Diego toward San Francisco Bay in 1769, diarist Fray Juan Crespi noted on July 28 that while camped along what is now called the Santa Ana River, ". . . we experienced here a horrifying earthquake that was repeated four times during the day. The first, which was the most violent, happened at one in the afternoon, and the last one about four." Crespi's vocabulary did not include "seismic waves" or "aftershocks," but he knew what he felt—a quake of M5.0 - 6.0. Aftershocks apparently continued for a week, for on August 1, the Crespi diary reads, "At 10 in the morning the earth trembled. The shock was repeated with violence in the afternoon, and one hour afterward we experienced another."

Because development occurred slowly in the state during the next century, reliable earthquake reports are scarce until the 1850s. Then the population upsurge after the Gold Rush brought increased interest in California's

State law now prohibits new construction directly on top of a known active fault. In this housing development east of San Francisco Bay, structures are set back from the fault. The fault is covered by a greenbelt (top to bottom of photo). More information on state laws is on page 127. Photo Akira Ono, Asahi Shimbun.

Newspapers published after the 1906 San Francisco earthquake described the destruction in emotional detail. The April 19 Extra published by the Oakland Tribune (right) describes the chaos caused by the shaking and fire, and the first attempts to help the citizens begin their recovery. Photographs were not available until April 20.

geology. The quake of 1857 (see page 89) sounded the first alarm bell, and the quake of 1906 (see page 96) brought the whole world's attention to California as Earthquake Country.

Today, every major shake in a California metropolitan area is chronicled throughout the world, complete with harrowing stories of human misery and heroism. Satellite television coverage has added to the reputation. Because the 1989 Loma Prieta earthquake struck at the start of a World Series baseball game, San Francisco was filled with TV cameras and crews, along with mobile units, blimps, and more than enough commentators. Millions of people who live far from California, and have never felt the earth tremble, were able to experience the thrill of an earthquake vicariously. They saw the devastation, listened to the victims and watched emergency rescue operations, live and in full color.

The spotlight is not likely to abandon California any time soon. We may well be in the midst of the most important chapter of California's seismic history. Between 1971 and 1994—only 23 years—nine significant earthquakes tested our assumptions on the location and nature of faults, ground motion and the stability of our man-made structures. Eight of the nine quakes were compressed into the period between May 1983 and January, 1994, for a remarkably short 15-month average interval:

1. The 1983 Coalinga and 1987 Whittier quakes sharply focused on the dangers of hidden thrust faults and provided the evidence needed to recognize their surface manifestations.

2. Sources of the 1971 San Fernando and 1994 Northridge quakes were eerily close together, illustrating how closely packed are the faults in and around the Los Angeles basin.

3. The 1989 Loma Prieta quake opened our eyes to the dangers faced by the entire San Francisco Bay Area from a movement on any one segment of its multiple fault zones.

4. The 1980 and 1992 Humboldt County quakes turned new attention to the complex geology and dangerous potential of fault zones in the Pacific Northwest.

5. The 1987 Superstition Hills and 1992 Landers quakes were unusual because their complex surface-rupture patterns extended over multiple faults.

It would be comforting to Californians if the seismic past was the key to the future, and scientists could provide times and dates of the next major quakes. In reality, earthquakes of destructive magnitude have occurred on an erratic schedule and in a frustrating variety of locations. This makes prediction difficult. It also complicates the best efforts to design and build earthquake-resistant structures.

Each new event receives more thorough analysis, resulting in new adjustments in engineering standards and building codes, more preventive safety measures, and better emergency procedures. Still, Mother Nature always has more tricks up her sleeve than mere mortals can easily forecast and conquer.

Any Californian who knows even a few facts about the state's seismicity realizes the term *earthquake* can mean many things. Most often, it refers to a few seconds of shaking that rarely does anything worse than rattle windows, crack a little plaster or occasionally knock down an older brick chimney.

Earthquakes of this size are so common in some coastal areas that those who follow the newspapers regularly soon fancy themselves experts on the subject. After every shake, magnitude numbers are repeated and compared like so many hat sizes. The latest rattlings and rollings are compared to "the last big one." These shakes provide a few thrills and plenty of conversation, but little to worry about.

However, for the resident of Sylmar in 1994, Santa Cruz in 1989, or Santa Rosa in 1906, *earthquake* meant something entirely different. It is a terrible force that sends violent convulsions through the earth, shakes buildings to the ground in seconds, and causes complete panic in otherwise rational people. These quakes leave indelible impressions on the state's landscape, its commercial life, and its residents.

A gentle swaying of the house and a few rattling dishes are one thing. But when the brick facings of downtown stores fall into the street on top of parked cars, gas mains break, and your own garage roof collapses a few feet from the back door, your life is suddenly on the line.

There's a lot to be said for being a "survivor," with your own stories to be repeated at the slightest provocation at dinner parties. And despite isolated reports of looting and price-gouging, there is always a greater sense of community and cooperation during the first scary days after a major quake.

A large earthquake often becomes a key date in the entire life span of those who "ride it out," the kind of event that sticks in your mind for the rest of your life. San Franciscans who can't remember what they had for lunch yesterday can tell you exactly where they were and what they were doing at 5 p.m. on October 17, 1989.

Earthquakes are perfect myth-makers. The source is unseen, the force appears with no warning, it appears capricious in its destruction, and then it is gone again in a minute. The next one may come the same day, next week—or not for 20 years. The event is completely out of anyone's control, and the sense of helplessness can be overwhelming. The fear, the fascination, and the emotional trauma are all understandable. How can you run from something you can't see?

There are no preliminary signals—no way to know where the quake will strike or how long it will last. And while the heaviest shaking is going on, you can't locate the source—marked contrasts to other natural disasters. Those who witnessed the Mt. St. Helen eruption or Hurricane Andrew or the upper Mississippi River floods had fair warning of what was coming, and could see the source of all the death and destruction. Those who were

The best place to see surface features of the San Andreas Fault is in Carrizo Plain (see page 47). The fault itself is recognizable as a pronounced trough cutting through the low hills. Detailed features such as escarpments and offset streams are very common and can be easily viewed from the area's system of unpaved roads. Photo courtesy California Department of Water Resources.

Frank Leslie's Illustrated Newspaper, opposite page, published in New York City, gave extensive and detailed coverage to the Charleston, South Carolina, earthquake of September 1, 1886. The isoseismal map (see page 67 for explanation of intensities) indicates that strong shock waves were felt as far east as St. Louis and as far north as Detroit. Very few structures in Charleston itself were spared significant damage. Major damage also was reported in Alabama, Ohio, Kentucky, Virginia and West Virginia. Death toll was estimated at 60.

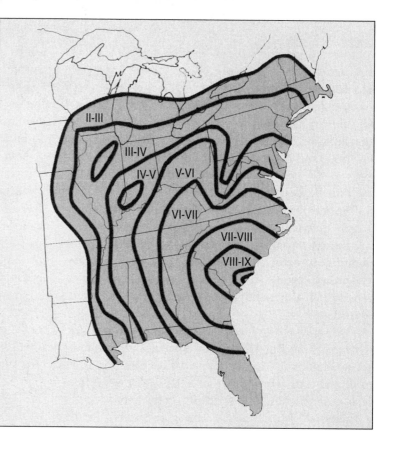

THE PANIC-STRICKEN CITIZENS SEEKING REFUGE ON BATTERY PLACE.

Librarians all over the Los Angeles area were faced with scenes like this on February 9, 1971, after the San Fernando earthquake. Weeks of repair, recataloging, and restacking were required to make the Central Library functional again. Items most likely to fall during even moderate earthquakes are those stacked loosely on shelves, such as bottles and cans in a grocery store, or books on a shelf. Los Angeles Times photo.

surprised by the 1994 Northridge earthquake could only feel the earth rock and roll, watch the structures around them crumble and fall, and just wonder "What in the world is happening?"

The shaky Californian who has just survived one of these scary jolts and looks here or anywhere else for some way to escape future danger will be acutely disappointed. Unless you choose the lifestyle of a hermit on a remote Sierra mountain top, you cannot live in California and escape earthquake danger. The most practical attitude is to admit that California *is* Earthquake Country and will continue to be so far beyond our lifetimes.

While nothing can be done to eliminate causes, much can be done about effects. Only one in 10,000 California fault movements ever does any great damage, but we should always be ready for the day when that almost casual shaking under our feet suddenly becomes the greatest earthquake of the century.

EARTHQUAKES AROUND THE WORLD

The U.S. Geological Survey's National Earthquake Information Center monitors seismic activity around the world. This is the average earthquake frequency worldwide, by magnitude, based on observations since 1900:

Magnitude	Annual Average
8.0 & higher	1
7-7.9	18
6-6.9	120
5-5.9	800
4-4.9	6,200 (est.)
3-3.9	49,000 (est.)
3.0 & lower	1,000,000+ (est.)

San Gorgonio Pass in Southern California is a giant, narrow block "left behind" when movements over millions of years along active branches of the San Andreas fault zone elevated mountain ranges on either side. Similar, smaller blocks characterize terrain along other parts of the fault (see page 37). Fairchild Aerial Surveys photo.

TIMING IS EVERYTHING

Three charts on the following pages show the years, dates, and times of day for California earthquakes with magnitudes of M6.5 or greater, from 1800 to January, 1996.

The lists are somewhat arbitrary because data used to compute magnitudes is open to different interpretations, and more than one magnitude scale is in use (see page 61). In most cases, moment magnitude is used, because it is the most reliable for large quakes.

Californians have benefited because many of the state's greatest earthquakes occurred when schools were not in session, office buildings were empty and traffic on freeways was relatively light. This advantageous timing is significant in the low death totals recorded in earthquakes here compared to the rest of the world (see page 137).

It is easy to play the "what-if" game when assessing earthquakes past and future:

What if the great 1906 earthquake had occurred at 10:13 a.m. when the coastal cities were busy with the commerce of the day, instead of 5:13 a.m.?

What if the 1933 Long Beach quake had occurred three hours earlier, at 2:54 p.m., when badly designed and poorly constructed schools were filled with children?

What if the 1994 Northridge quake had shaken the Los Angeles basin not at 4:31 a.m., when everything was quiet, but just a few hours later at 9:31 a.m.?

What if another earthquake the size of the 1906 event strikes the San Francisco Bay Area in early afternoon when millions of people are in high-rise office buildings, in schools built on or near the San Andreas fault zone or on the transbay bridges?

One of the most perplexing problems facing geologists and seismologists is the stubborn refusal of major quakes to occur on any predictable timetable (see page 121). History teaches us *what* to expect, but not *when* to expect it. The charts are fascinating in the patterns that emerge. But reader beware—use the numbers to marvel at the past, not to predict the future.

WHAT'S THE YEAR?

This list indicates the variations in intervals between major quakes, and emphasizes the difficulties involved in using past records to predict future events.

The average interval is slightly more than three years; actual intervals range from a maximum of 24 years (1812-1836), down to less than 24 hours. Because of the state's sparse development, some M6.5 quakes may have gone unreported during the 1812-1836 gap.

Two significant clusters are the 16 quakes between 1890 and 1917 (37 years), and the 11 events between 1968 and 1994 (26 years).

Decade	Earthquakes
1800	
	1800 San Diego, M6.5
1810	
	1812 Santa Barbara Channel, M7.0
	1812 Wrightwood, M7.0
1820	
1830	
	1836 Hayward, M6.8
	1838 San Francisco Peninsula, M7.0
1840	
1850	
	1852 Colorado River, M6.5
	1857 Tejon Pass, M7.8
1860	
	1868 Hayward, M7.0

1870	
	1872 Owens Valley (3 events: M7.6, M6.6, M6.5)
	1873 Crescent City, M6.7
1880	
1890	
	1890 San Diego County, M6.6
	1892 California-Mexico border, M7.0
	1897 Gilroy, M6.5
	1898 Mare Island, M6.5
	1898 Mendocio County, M6.5
	1899 Hemet, M6.9
	1899 Eureka, M7.0
1900	
	1901 Parkfield, M6.5
	1906 San Francisco, M7.7

Opposite page: International coverage of the 1989 Loma Prieta earthquake featured only two images—the Marina District fire in San Francisco (left) and the collapsed East Bay freeway viaduct (right). This left TV viewers and newspaper readers far from California with two mistaken impressions: First, that the epicentral area was near San Francisco, rather than in the Santa Cruz mountains, and second, that all of San Francisco and Oakland had sustained disastrous damage. In reality, the most widespread effects were in the Santa Cruz mountains and the towns around Monterey Bay. Serious damage in San Francisco and the East Bay was restricted to limited areas with specific problems (see page 112). Cypress Viaduct photo, Howard G. Wilshire, U. S. Geological Survey; fire photo, University of California EERC Library.

The 1933 Long Beach earthquake (see page 98) was one of the first events to illustrate what happens when a relatively minor fault movement occurs under a highly developed area with poor soils and inadequate construction techniques. Compton (above) and Long Beach were hardest-hit areas but damage occurred throughout the Los Angeles basin. Photo courtesy Wilfrid N. Ball Collection.

1908 Inyo County, M6.5

1910

1911 Coyote, M6.6

1915 Eureka, M6.5

1918 San Jacinto, M6.8

1918 Eureka, M6.5

1920

1923 Cape Mendocino, M7.2

1927 Lompoc, M7.2

1930

1940

1940 Imperial Valley, M7.1

1941 Cape Mendocino, M6.6

1942 Fish Creek Mountains, M6.5

1950

1952 Kern County, M7.5

1954 Eureka, M6.6

1960

1968 Borrego Mountain, M6.5

1970

1971 San Fernando, M6.7

1979 Imperial Valley, M6.5

1980

1980 Humboldt County, M7.2

1983 Coalinga, M6.5

1987 Superstition Hills, M6.6

1989 Loma Prieta, M6.9

1990

1992 Landers, M7.3

1992 Cape Mendocino (3 events: M7.1, M6.7, M6.6)

1994 Northridge, M6.7

2000

WHAT'S THE DATE?

Similarly, dates of major quakes are not distributed evenly over the calendar, and the pattern invites speculation:

1. One of Northern California's favorite myths—"April is earthquake month"—turns out to have some validity. Almost 20% of the events listed here occurred in that one 30-day period.
2. Geographic distribution is about even between Northern California (20) and Southern California (23, including Parkfield and Coalinga). Quakes east of the Sierra Nevada (3) belong in a separate category.
3. Historical data cannot be used to predict future events, but it seems that August and September are the seismically safest times to take a California vacation.

The exact date of the June 1838 San Francisco Peninsula earthquake is unknown.

JANUARY
- 9   1857 Tejon Pass, M7.8
- 17   1994 Northridge, M6.7
- 22   1923 Cape Mendocino, M7.2

FEBRUARY
- 9   1890 San Diego County, M6.6
- 9   1941 Cape Mendocino, M6.6
- 9   1971 San Fernando, M6.7
- 23   1892 California-Mexico border, M7.0

MARCH
- 2   1901 Parkfield, M6.5
- 26   1872 Owens Valley (2 events: M7.6, M6.5)
- 30   1898 Mare Island, M6.5

APRIL
- 8   1968 Borrego Mountain, M6.5
- 11   1872 Owens Valley, M6.6
- 14   1898 Mendocino County, M6.5
- 16   1899 Eureka, M7.0
- 18   1906 San Francisco, M7.7
- 21   1918 San Jacinto, M6.8
- 25   1992 Cape Mendocino, M7.1
- 26   1992 Cape Mendocino (2 events: M6.6, M6.7)

MAY
- 2   1983 Coalinga, M6.5
- 18   1940 Imperial Valley, M7.1

JUNE
- 10   1836 Hayward, M6.8
- 20   1897 Gilroy, M6.5
- 28   1992 Landers, M7.3
- ??   1838 San Francisco Peninsula, M7.0

JULY
- 1   1911 Coyote, M6.6
- 14   1918 Eureka, M6.5
- 21   1952 Kern County, M7.5

AUGUST

SEPTEMBER

OCTOBER
- 15   1979 Imperial Valley, M6.5
- 17   1989 Loma Prieta, M6.9
- 21   1868 Hayward, M7.0
- 21   1942 Fish Creek Mountains, M6.5

NOVEMBER
- 4   1908 Inyo County, M6.5
- 4   1927 Lompoc, M7.2
- 8   1980 Humboldt County, M7.2
- 22   1800 San Diego, M6.5
- 22   1873 Crescent City, M6.7
- 24   1987 Superstition Hills, M6.6
- 29   1852 Colorado River, M6.5

DECEMBER
- 8   1812 Wrightwood, M7.0
- 21   1812 Santa Barbara Channel M7.0
- 21   1954 Eureka, M6.6
- 25   1899 Hemet, M6.9
- 31   1915 Eureka, M6.5

Prior to 1906, the Hayward earthquake of October 21, 1868, was referred to as "the great earthquake" in the San Francisco Bay Area. It caused a surface rupture along the Hayward Fault (see page 43) and did substantial damage on both sides of the Bay. The San Leandro courthouse was one of many public buildings that were not designed to withstand major quakes because of the limited seismic knowledge of the time. The 1868 event was significant not only in its own right but also as part of a pattern that makes the Bay Area susceptible to a significant quake in the future (see page 126).

The 1906 San Francisco earthquake and fire ranks as the most significant seismic event in California's recorded history. It focused international attention on the state's susceptibility to major earthquakes. As a result of this quake, ongoing scientific efforts were initiated to understand the nature of the San Andreas and related faults. One of the greatest fears among scientists today is that a repeat of this quake will cause major loss of life and property damage in the Bay Area's heavily populated areas (see page 126).

Freeway design standards and construction techniques were significantly modified because of damage sustained during earthquakes of the 1980s and 1990s. This elevated structure near Eureka collapsed in the November 8, 1980 Humboldt County quake of magnitude 7.2. Standards for new construction, and the retrofitting of older freeways, are intended to resist the dangerous and powerful combination of vertical, horizontal, and twisting motions resulting from complex shock waves generated by a major fault movement (see page 72). Retrofitting of older freeways throughout the state accelerated after the 1994 Northridge quake. Photo courtesy University of California EERC Library.

WHAT'S THE TIME?

Pacific Standard Times are listed; when quakes occurred while Daylight Savings Time was in effect, PDT is indicated in parentheses.

While future quakes may not follow this same pattern, look at these interesting distributions:

1. Almost two-thirds occurred during the 14-hour period between 6 p.m. and 8 a.m., when family members are most likely to be home.
2. The hours of greatest frequency are 4-8 a.m.
3. You can probably enjoy your lunch in peace—there hasn't been a large quake between noon and 2 p.m. since 1897.

Times for earthquakes before 1906 are estimates based on anecdotal records. The San Francisco Peninsula quake of 1838 (M7.0), is known only to have occurred sometime in the afternoon, and therefore is not listed.

12 MIDNIGHT
12:37 1908 Inyo County, M6.5

1 AM
1:04 1923 Cape Mendocino, M7.2

1:44 1941 Cape Mendocino, M6.6

2
2:27 1980 Humboldt County, M7.2

2:30 1872 Owens Valley, M7.6

3
3:18 (4:18 PDT) 1992 Cape Mendocino, M6.6

3:52 (4:52 PDT) 1952 Kern County, M7.5

3:58 (4:58 PDT) 1992 Landers, M7.3

4
4:06 1890 San Diego County, M6.6

4:20 1915 Eureka, M6.5

4:25 1899 Hemet, M6.9

4:31 1994 Northridge, M6.7

5
5:13 1906 San Francisco, M7.7

5:16 1987 Superstition Hills, 6.6

5:40 1899 Eureka, M7.0

5:50 1927 Lompoc, M7.2

6
6:00 1971 San Fernando, M6.7

6:06 1872 Owens Valley, M6.5

7
7:00 1812 Wrightwood, M7.0

7:30 1836 Hayward, M6.8

7:53 1868 Hayward, M7.0

8
8:22 (9:22 PDT) 1942 Fish Creek Mountains, M6.5

8:24 1857 Tejon Pass, M7.8

9

10
10:06 (11:06 PDT) 1992 Cape Mendocino, M7.1

11
11:00 1812 Santa Barbara Channel, M7.0

11:00 1872 Owens Valley, M6.6

11:56 1954 Eureka, M6.6

12 NOON
12:00 1852 Colorado River, M6.5

12:14 1897 Gilroy, M6.5

1 PM
1:30 1800 San Diego, M6.5

2
2:00 1911 Coyote, M6.6

2:32 (3:32 PDT) 1918 San Jacinto, M6.8

2:42 (3:42 PDT) 1983 Coalinga, M6.5

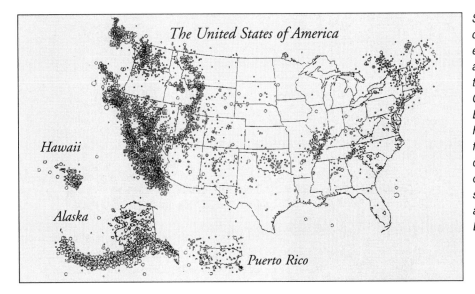

The United States of America

Hawaii

Alaska

Puerto Rico

Seismicity map indicates epicenters of all major recorded earthquakes between 1899 and 1990. It clearly shows the pattern that earns California the reputation as Earthquake Country. However, the potential exists for significant intraplate earthquakes in Nevada, throughout the Rocky Mountain states, in southern Missouri and in northern New England.

3

3:16 (4:16 PDT) 1979
Imperial Valley, M6.5

4

4:04 (5:04 PDT) 1989
Loma Prieta, M6.9

4:23 (5:23 PDT) 1918
Eureka, M6.5

5

6

6:28 1968 Borrego
Mountain, M6.5

7

8

8:36 1940 Imperial
Valley, M7.1

9

9:00 1873 Crescent City, M6.7

10

11

11:07 1898 Mendocino
County, M6.5

11:20 1892 California-
Mexico border, M 7.0

11:41 (12:41 A.M. PDT)
1992 Cape Mendocino, M6.6

11:43 1898 Mare Island, M6.5

11:45 1901 Parkfield, M6.5

A bizarre effect of the 1952 earthquake (see page 100) resulted from two commonly observed earth movements: A wall uplifted from violent vertical motion and the the railroad track was simultaneously buckled by ground compression (see page 81). When the wall returned to its original position, it trapped the buckled rails underneath. G. I. Smith photo.

Damage from the 1906 San Francisco earthquake extended for hundreds of miles along the San Andreas Fault zone (see page 96). One of the hardest-hit areas was Stanford University. There, a statue of Louis Agassiz was shaken from its perch on the main quadrangle to plunge headlong into the pavement below. Photo courtesy University of California EERC Library.

THE JANUARY 17, 1995, EARTHQUAKE IN KOBE, JAPAN

The disastrous M6.8 earthquake in Japan on January 17, 1995 was similar to California earthquakes of the recent past. It serves as a model of what might happen in a future quake located in a densely populated area such as the San Francisco Bay Area.

The Japanese quake originated on a mapped fault that had been quiet in recent times, with only one recorded quake above M6 back in 1916. Research after the 1995 event indicates there may have been a great quake of about M8.0 about 1500, but nothing significant since. This history caused some Japanese seismologists to predict in 1994 that an event as devastating as California's Northridge quake could never happen in the Kobe area.

The Kobe quake occurred at 5:46 a.m.; the hours of greatest frequency in California are 4-8 a.m. (see page 12). And, as has been the situation in California, the Japanese were extremely fortunate that the main shock came when most citizens were asleep rather than in offices and schools. The 6.8 magnitude was typical of the recent damaging Southern California quakes.

The death toll approached 6,000, many more than in any California quake, with extensive property damage in the epicental area. As in California, the greatest damage and loss of life occurred in areas of soft soils and dense populations. Older buildings sustained the worst damage, especially wood structures with tile roofs and little lateral support. High-rise buildings performed very well, as did virtually all structures constructed since stiff building codes took effect in 1981.

The center of greatest damage, Port Island, was a huge area of landfill and alluvium, developed since the late 1960s.

Extensive commercial development included port facilities, industrial structures and thousands of apartments with about 17,000 residents. Port and ferry terminals were closed by the quake, and a major elevated expressway built in the 1960s collapsed in five places. Freeways in general did not do as well as expected in the areas of heaviest shaking. The only highway open between Kobe and Osaka was closed to incoming cars; trucks had to use an alternate narrow road.

The right-lateral strike-slip motion (see page 29) caused a 30-mile long subsurface rupture. The hypocenter was about 12.5 miles deep, under the island of Awaji, 20 miles from Kobe. The rupture propagated in two directions, one of which went directly under Kobe. Shaking lasted more than 20 seconds, typical of recent Southern California quakes but much shorter than we can expect in a repeat of the 1906 quake (page 125).

This quake reportedly produced exceptionally strong vertical shaking, also typical of recent Southern California quakes. More than a dozen significant aftershocks occurred in the first three hours, and 600 the first day, a predictable pattern.

All major utilities were crippled. More than 900,000 households lost electricity and gas. Water was shut off to 60,000 households. More than 120,000 people sought temporary shelter the night after the quake. Fire was a major cause of damage and death, as it always is in Japanese quakes because of the common use of small kerosene, gas and electric heaters that are easily toppled. Firefighters had a difficult time because the supply of water was curtailed by broken mains, and because many streets were blocked by rubble. This is similar to the experience reported in San Francisco after the 1989 quake.

Damage patterns from the Kobe earthquake paralleled the experience of California communities with similar characteristics. Combined vertical and horizontal stresses placed on older structures, especially those on alluvial soils, was disastrous. Sections of an elevated freeway (opposite page) buckled and fell. Inadequately reinforced structures toppled. Intensities were amplified by liquifaction in the epicental area. Firefighting and rescue attempts (above) were hampered by major dislocation of major utilities. Akira Ono, Asahi Shimbun photos.

Earthquakes of the last two decades prompted dramatic improvements in the ability of public agencies to deal with the catastrophic results. This family spent a night in Granada Hills High School, one of five emergency centers set up by the Red Cross in the San Fernando Valley following the 1971 quake. At the personal level, California's residents can do a great deal to minimize damage to their residences. They can prepare their families and friends to react quickly and safely after the shaking stops (see page 134). Pacific Telephone photo.

Vehicles parked on city streets often take a beating if nearby buildings are faced with unreinforced bricks and masonry that topple quickly and easily under earthquake stress. This car was parked on Tehachapi's main street at the time of the 1952 quake (see page 100). Open-faced buildings in the background illustrate how fronts peel away even though basic structures remain standing. Photo by Edwin A. Verner.

Some areas directly on top of California's active fault systems, such as the section of northern San Mateo County shown above, are covered by extensive commercial and residential developments. A repeat of the 1906 earthquake, with the same surface rupture and widespread shaking, would place many of these structures and their occupants at considerable risk. This problem is not restricted to the San Andreas Fault; the complex system of hidden thrust faults in Southern California underlies major population centers (see page 27). Robert E. Wallace photo.

The 1992 Landers earthquake (see page 115) was characterized by spectacular surface ruptures, some of which ran directly through man-made structures. Scientists have been able to use information gathered during and after this very significant quake for a better understanding of the nature of fault movements. Photo by W. A. Bryant.

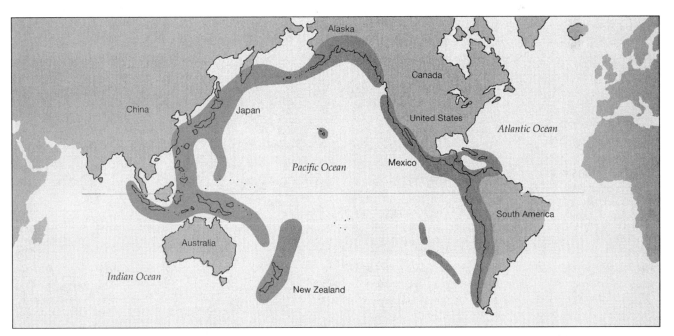

A lion's share of the world's earthquakes originate in the related group of faults that loops around the Pacific Basin. This "ring of fire" is related to the movement of hugh plates—blocks of the earth's crust that bump and slide past each other like gigantic ice floes.

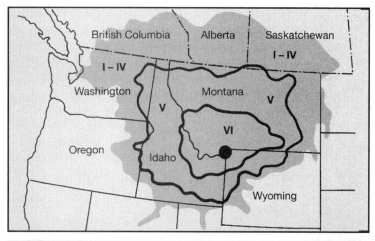

Shock waves from the 1959 Hegben Lake, Montana, quake spread over most of the Pacific Northwest (see page 67 for explanations of intensities expressed in roman numerals). A lengthy surface rupture and landsliding closed many roads. A new "Quake Lake" was created when a slide backed up Madison River waters to cover parts of State Highway 1. Photos courtesy University of California EERC Library.

1964 Alaska earthquake was characterized by severe landsliding and secondary earth slumping. This caused the Turnagain Heights residential area in Anchorage (above) to slide out into the sea, and turned the 4th Avenue section (right) into chaos.

In 1964, Kodiak's seaside area (above) was devastated. Slumping cracked highways in Portage (right). The resulting tsunami swept down the coast of North America and caused considerable damage at several California points, especially Crescent City (below). For more information on tsunamis, see page 83. Photos courtesy University of California EERC Library.

The 1971 San Fernando earthquake attracted major international attention because of its widespread damage (Olive View County Hospital shown above) and the important new seismological data gathered on instrumental records. Photo by R. Kachadoorian.

Not all seismic damage results from earthquakes; slow creep along certain sections of faults causes streets to crack and curbs to bend and eventually break. The streets of Hollister, shown above, have been subjected to long-term creep that may provide clues to the size and location of future quakes (see page 81). Photo courtesy of University of California EERC Library.

Why California Has Earthquakes

Chapter 2

The San Andreas Fault cuts a spectacular swath through Carrizo Plain, a dry and desolate area of central California. Because of arid conditions, many fault features–some created by the 1857 earthquake–remain well preserved. Photo courtesy University of California EERC Library.

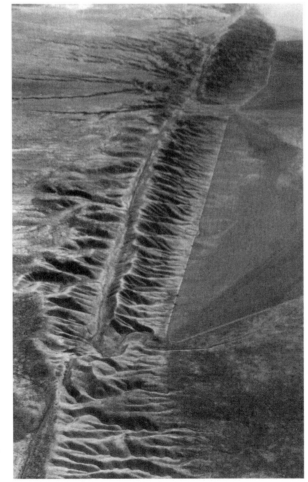

Since the 1960s, scientists have made great progress in understanding how the earth's topographic features have evolved. It was long theorized that an underlying process distributed the land masses around the globe and created the major continents and oceans. The theory was codified into Plate Tectonics after analysis of sea-floor geomagnetic anomalies revealed breaks in the earth's crust that marked the boundaries of huge chunks of the earth's surface. The patterns of earthquake and volcanic activity can be explained by movements along these plate boundaries.

Plate Tectonics

Here is a simplified version of Plate Tectonics as it relates to California:

The *lithosphere*, the earth's outer shell, is not a single, unified layer. It is composed of 12 large, rigid plates and several smaller plates. The largest plates cover millions of square miles. They may support continents, oceans or a combination of the two.

These plates are not stationary. Some internal global force, probably a combination of gravity and heat convection, keeps them in constant motion, sliding over a deep, hot, semi-plastic layer just under the lithosphere. Boundaries between the plates are planes of weakness. It is here that the plate movements can be observed by great geologic activity—rising mountain ranges, subsiding oceanic trenches, active volcanoes and violent earthquakes. Near the surface, where rocks are brittle, the planes separating the plates are called *faults*. At greater depths, the relative plate movements are accomplished by the flow of heated rock, and no faults are formed.

Plot the earth's major earthquakes and volcanic eruptions over the last 500 years, and the major plates are automatically defined. Earthquakes occur away from plate boundaries. But to generate a series of significant quakes over a short geologic time period, large amounts of strain must be able to accumulate along a plane that can serve as a relief mechanism.

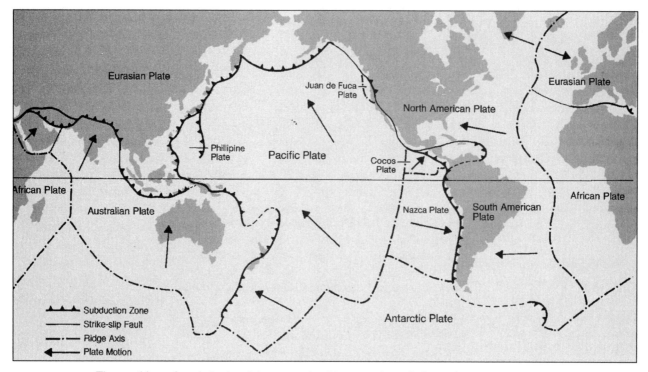

The earth's surface is broken into a mosaic of large and small plates that are constantly in motion. Boundaries between these plates are the location of active, long-term tectonic activity. The San Andreas fault separates the Pacific and North American plates and is the best-exposed strike-slip fault in the world. "Ridge axis" is the term used to define an underwater boundary between diverging plates.

As the plates move in relation to each other along the faults, they do one of three things:

1. They converge (bump into each other), with one plate usually sliding beneath the other. The plate that is forced downward is the thinner and heavier. It is always made up of ocean floor that is denser than continents and therefore tends to sink beneath the lighter continental rocks. The area where one plate slides beneath another is called a *subduction zone.* Such zones are found in the Pacific Northwest, Japan, the Alaskan Aleutian Islands, and the west coast of South America.

Subduction zones are very active, producing 80% of the world's earthquakes, plus dramatic volcanic eruptions. Volcanoes are created when the plunging slab is heated as it enters the deeper levels of the crust, causing fingers of magma to rise to the surface.

Off the coasts of Chile and Peru, one huge plate is being shoved into a deep trench, helping to build the Andes mountains and causing tremendous earthquakes, including the largest ever recorded—M9. 5 in 1960. The Himalayan Mountains are a striking example of what happens when two plates bump into each other. Neither one sinks, and the crust is pushed upward over millions of years. Subduction zones are the only regions where earthquakes occur at depths of

more than about 20 miles beneath the surface. The Bolivian earthquake of June, 1994, originated at a depth of 400 miles.

2. They diverge (pull away from each other). This motion usually starts in ocean floors. As plates diverge from each other, hot material from the earth's interior oozes up in the trench, solidifies, and becomes part of the plates on either side. New material moves outward as though transported by a conveyor belt. Older material at the other edge of the plate moves downward under an adjacent plate in a subduction zone. Among the largest spreading centers are the mid-Atlantic ridge, Africa's rift valley, and the Gorda Ridge off California's Mendocino Coast.

3. They slip (move laterally past each other), which is the situation along most of the west coast of California. The Pacific Plate is made up of the northern Pacific Ocean, a slice of far-western California (including the Monterey Bay area, San Luis Obispo, the Santa Barbara coast, the Los Angeles basin, and San Diego) and Baja California. The North American plate includes the rest of North America and the western half of the Atlantic Ocean. They slip past each other laterally for the most part. The plane on which most of the motion occurs is the San Andreas fault system, one of the best exposed

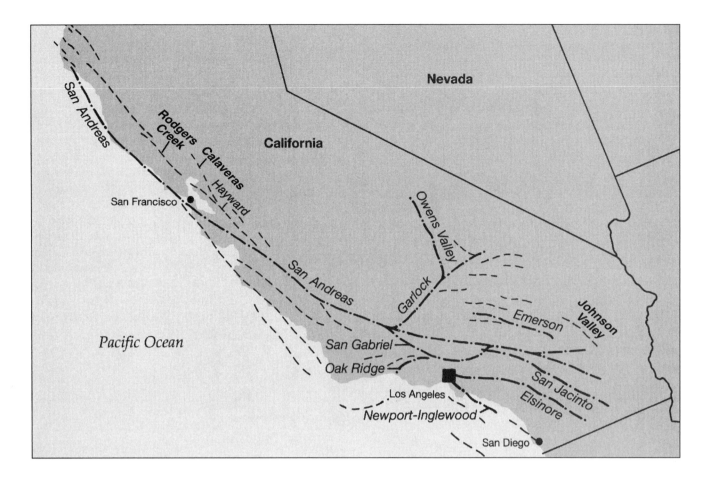

SIGNIFICANT FAULTS IN CALIFORNIA

This map locates faults that created most of the large earthquakes in the state's recorded history. Hundreds of others are capable of producing major quakes at any time.

San Andreas fault is the most publicized rift in California; it is by far the longest in the state and annually produces dozens of earthquakes. Despite its long-term significance in the state's seismic history, the San Andreas should not be blamed for every tremor. Actually, the main branch of this great fault has been relatively quiet in the second half of the 20th century, and most of the state's significant quakes have originated on other faults.

Hayward fault, despite its distinctive name, is really a major branch of the San Andreas zone. The fault has played a significant role in the geologic development of the San Francisco Bay area. It has given birth to several large tremors during recorded history. Related fracture zones include the

Calaveras fault to the east and the Rodgers Creek fault to the north.

Owens Valley fault zone is the source of significant movements that created the escarpment that forms the eastern edge of the Sierra (see page 35). The great 1872 quake originated here.

Garlock, the second-largest fault in the state, has been the source of significant quakes that helped define the landscape (page 49). Strangely, not a single great quake during recorded history can be blamed on this great fracture zone.

San Gabriel fault extends from Fort Tejon, epicenter of the great 1857 quake on the San Andreas fault, south to the Pasadena area, where it intersects with the Santa Monica fault.

Elsinore fault is the westernmost of the several major branches of the very complex San Andreas fault zone in southern California; it has been uncharacteristically quiet during the last two centuries.

San Jacinto fault may be the most active branch of the San Andreas zone; it has been the source of many important quakes in the past 200 years. Land forms along its route give ample testimony to its long-term significance on the state's topography.

Oak Ridge fault was the source of the 1994 Northridge quake; its character is complex and not completely understood or mapped.

Newport-Inglewood fault was unknown until 1920, when a small quake indicated the location of an active break along the coast. Then, in 1933, the Long Beach earthquake verified the existence of the fault and its potential.

Emerson/Johnson Valley fault zone is very complex; some branches were unrecognized until the 1992 Landers quake revealed the extent of the broad fracture zone.

At 5:12 a.m. on April 18, 1906, impressive sandstone gates still guarded the entrance to Stanford University. A minute later, only a heap of rubble was left.

tectonic-plate boundaries in the world.

All these plate movements are complex and interrelated. The aggregate effect over the million-year periods that characterize the geologic time scale, is a slow, continuous re-configuration of the landscape of the world with constant creation, distortion and destruction of new lithosphere. Mountain ranges are elevated, valleys grow wider and deeper, coastlines change and the world's topography continues to evolve.

Since the initial separation of land and water during the Earth's early history, the continental land masses have been joined and separated more than once. The present configuration of the continents began to take shape about 200-million years ago when a great supercontinent began to break into the pieces that form the current plate configurations.

Evidence for this break-up is not hard to find. For example, geologic and fossil records—and a cursory look at a world map—indicate that the east coast of South America once fit together with the west coast of Africa; northwestern Africa was joined to the Gulf Coast area of North America. When the two continents parted, Africa left behind pieces of lithosphere that became part of the southeastern United States. Recent, detailed measurements provided by the Global Positioning Satellite System (see page 130) confirms the movement patterns suggested by geologic evidence.

The size and nature of the plates are changed by all this creation and destruction of lithosphere. At this moment in geologic time, the Pacific plate appears to be diminishing in size, while others—including the North American plate—are growing larger.

Plates move just about as fast as your fingernails grow—a few inches a year, about 10-12 feet a century. This may not seem like much, but a 65-year-old native of New York now lives about six feet farther away from his counterpart in Paris than he did at the time of his birth because of the spreading center in the middle of the Atlantic Ocean. Similarly, residents of San Francisco and Los Angeles are moving closer together at about the same rate because of horizontal movements along the boundary of the Pacific and North American plates.

The plates move smoothly at depths greater than 15 miles. Nearer the surface, frictional resistance along the faults causes a more erratic "stick-slip" motion. Where the plates become "stuck" or locked together because of this great pressure, stress accumulates until it is strong enough to snap. These sudden movements along the boundary faults produce a quick, sudden movement along the weakest point—the fault at the boundaries—that sends out the shock waves we call an *earthquake*.

SLIP RATES

The rate at which rocks on one side of a fault segment move relative to the rocks on the other side over a century or longer is called the long-term, average slip rate. The most common method of measuring this slip rate is to find geologic features—stream beds, soil deposits, rock formations, lava flows—that have been broken and offset by movements along the fault. The amount of offset is divided by the age of the feature as determined by radiocarbon and other dating techniques. The result is the average slip rate per year. A stream bed that has been off-set 20 feet in the last 500 years indicates a slip rate of almost half an inch per year.

By using the slip rate, and the estimated average amount of slip per earthquake on any given fault segment, the recurrence interval for that segment can be estimated (see page 123).

California's longest fault, the San Andreas, is also its fastest moving, with a slip rate of 3/4 inch to almost two inches per year; it varies on different segments. For example, slip rates along the southern section are lower than those in its central section. Strain build-up in the south is accommodated by slip not only on the San Andreas fault but also on the San Jacinto and other, more westerly faults. More than a hundred other faults in the state have slip rates of at least one-third inch per year. See also page 38.

Trenching across active faults is an effective means of visibly verifying the amount of slip along individual segments. Photo by Glenn Borchardt.

Right-lateral movement along San Andreas fault in the 1906 earthquake caused a section of Inverness pier west of the fault to curve northward about 20 feet relative to foreground section east of the fault.

CAPE MENDOCINO'S "TRIPLE JUNCTION"

At the northern end of the San Andreas fault near Cape Mendocino is an unusual "triple junction" where three tectonic plates converge. The Pacific and North American plates are moving past each other, while the Gorda plate (the southern section of the Juan de Fuca plate) is sliding under the North American plate (see map at right).

The boundary between the Gorda/Juan de Fuca plates offshore and the North American plate onshore is known as the *Cascadia Subduction Zone.* This zone extends off the North American coast from Cape Mendocino to north of Vancouver Island. Inland from the Cascadia fault system, and related to it, are the Cascade range volcanoes.

North of the triple junction, the colliding North American and Gorda plates have created a band of folded and faulted crustal rocks, mostly off-shore. Near its southern end, the band curves onshore, exposing a belt of thrust faults along the Humboldt County coastline.

Paleoseismologic studies—plus effects of the 1992 Cape Mendocino earthquake—indicate that this is a very unstable area. There have been more than 60 quakes of M5.5 or greater since the mid-1800s and at least five large quakes of maybe M8+ or more during the past 2,000 years.

By analyzing historical accounts of a 9-foot tsunami that struck Japan on January 26, 1700, at about 9 p.m., researchers have tentatively assigned that date to the last big Pacific Northwest quake. No other earthquakes were reported around the Pacific Basin on that date. The only possible source is thought to have been the Cascadia Subduction Zone, known to have produced something major around that time. If the entire subduction zone ruptures once again, it would generate a quake to rank with the largest ever recorded. It probably would generate another major tsunami that would impact coastal areas around the entire Pacific Basin.

Role of The San Andreas Fault

Along the California coast, the Pacific Plate moves northwestward relative to the North American Plate, which appears to move southeastward. The rate of movement averages about two inches per year. Earthquakes and slow creep along the San Andreas fault system accommodate most of this movement; the Sierra Nevada and Basin and Range faults relieve some of it. The total deformation zone may extend from the Farallon Islands off San Francisco Bay all the way to Utah.

The lithosphere along the San Andreas fault is not typical. It varies in thickness from 12 to 40 miles, substantially less than the typical 40 to 60 mile thickness for most continental areas. Thinnest at both ends, at Cape Mendocino and in the Salton Sea trough, it is abnormally thick only under the Transverse Ranges (see page 28)

California's Fault Systems

Earthquakes resulting from fault movements along the boundary of the Pacific and North American plates have been an integral part of the geologic processes of the Western United States, and California in particular, since long before any human ever set foot in the Golden State. Ample geologic evidence makes it clear that the seismic history of the past 200 years reflects business as usual below California's scenic landscape. Indeed, without millions of years of earthquakes and crustal deformation, the state's topography might well resemble that of Kansas.

On either side of all of California's faults, pieces of landscape are irregularly elevated, tilted, folded and depressed. Each earthquake makes its contribution to the cumulative effect. Larger quakes can cause surprisingly large shifts. Bear Mountain in the Tehachapi Mountains was elevated three feet as a result of the 1952 Kern County quake; Oat Mountain in the Santa Susana Mountains was elevated about 15 inches by the 1994 Northridge quake.

Even smaller quakes have an effect. A relatively minor M6.0 magnitude quake on May 17, 1993, centered near the eastern California community of Independence about 30 miles northwest of Death Valley, caused California to grow an inch wider and an inch higher relative to the area in Nevada east of the fault. The M6.1 Whittier Narrows quake in 1978 raised the Montebello Hills by 1. 5 inches.

It is this seismically influenced landscape, and the related weather patterns, that have attracted millions of people to California. Today the earthquake-prone areas support some of the world's densest centers of population with all the trappings of modern civilization. Earthquakes alone are not the problem.

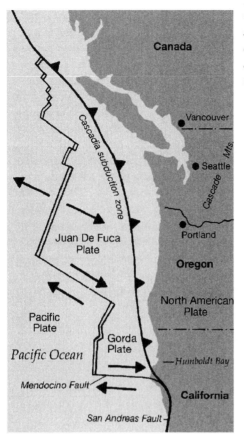

Generalized diagram shows main structures of complex tectonic area off the coast of the Pacific Northwest.

PALEOSEISMOLOGY

Paleoseismology is one of the key disciplines in modern earthquake research. It involves the study of events before the mid-1800s, as recorded by deformed strata in trenches, road cuts, stream beds and eroded surface topography. Exposed vertical surfaces often reveal offsets caused by ancient fault movements. These are carefully mapped and samples of the strata are gathered. Time intervals between the movements are estimated by using radiocarbon dating methods to establish the age of organic materials in each layer.

Paleoseismologic analysis has been a key element in estimating dates of prehistoric earthquakes in several areas, including those originating along the Mendocino coast, and on the San Andreas fault at Pallett Creek near Palmdale (see page 124).

Trenching is a primary method of establishing the exact location of faults under the Alquist-Priolo Earthquake Fault Zoning Act (see page 127). In general, more is learned about strike-slip faults by analyzing surface features; more is learned about dip-slip faults by trenching.

Homes, office buildings, schools, hospitals, dams, and freeways built during the state's development share responsibility for earthquake-related deaths and destruction. We cannot turn back the clock to 1800, so the only practical attitude for Californians is to learn to live with the state's faults. We need to be as prepared as possible for the inevitability of plate-tectonic activity and the earthquakes that result.

The state is interlaced with hundreds of identifiable faults; the most prominent are shown on page 23. The San Andreas is the longest and most active. However, the seismic history of the 20th Century shows that even the smaller, poorly defined and supposedly dormant faults can spring to life and cause as much damage as movements on their Big Brother.

Most of California's known faults are *dormant*, but some are described as *potentially active* by showing evidence of surface displacement in the last 1.6-million years (the Quaternary Epoch). Still others are *active*, with evidence of surface displacement in the last 11,000 years (the Holocene Period). A fault may creep slowly over long periods, may break at regular 100-300-year intervals, or may shift only once in 10,000 years. If that "once" happens in our lifetime, then we suffer the consequences.

The faults that caused the 1952 Tehachapi, 1971 San Fernando, 1983 Coalinga and 1987 Whittier Narrows quakes were unrecognized before they broke. Some faults that ruptured during the 1992 Landers quake may have appeared as insignificant features on geologic maps, but they—like hundreds of others—were ignored because there was no indication of any movement on them for the last 11,000 years, nor any recognizable clues that they were about to break.

Hidden Thrust Faults

The San Andreas fault has been extensively studied and mapped; its character is well known, if not completely understood. Faults characterized by vertical movements that break the surface (see page 29) have been recognized and analyzed for just as long.

Major earthquakes in the first half of the Twentieth Century were blamed on well-known major faults. It was assumed by many geologists that large California quakes, M6.0 or greater, could only be produced by faults that were delineated at the surface by features such as escarpments and major offsets in rock formations and drainage channels.

Since the 1970s, a new seismic threat has come to be fully recognized and feared—hidden thrust faults that lurk below the surface, with little or no recognizable surface expression. They, rather than the well-defined and well-mapped faults in the state, have caused Southern California's most damaging earthquakes in the second half of the 20th century.

Veteran's Hospital →

Pacoima Dam→

Every new major earth-quake contributes to the mountain-building process along the West Coast. Modern measuring tech-niques enable scientists to measure changes down to the inch. Here dust clouds rise over the southern California hills after one of the bigger aftershocks fol-lowing the 1971 Northridge quake. Veterans Hospital that sustained major dam-age is in the background; Pacoima Dam in fore-ground escaped unscathed. Gordon Air Photo.

Often called *blind faults,* these are really *hidden faults*—it is the observers who are blind because we can't see them. Hidden thrust faults are difficult to locate and map because they may be buried miles under the surface. In some places they lie beneath youthful folds, where sedimentary layers of rock have been folded, bent and pushed upward by compres-sional forces to create hills and adjacent basins. Surveys reveal that these folds tend to bend upward while the basins subside as stress develops before an earthquake.

During the first half of the 20th Century, most atten-tion was paid to the state's largest, most recognizable faults. Major-magnitude earthquakes were surprising-ly infrequent during the 1920s, 1930s, and 1940s (see page 8), and most were attributed to the San Andreas system and its many branches. The 1952 Kern County earthquake was the first California event to cause sci-entists to take a closer look at shallow dip-slip faults that were not clearly visible at the surface.

The 1971 San Fernando quake provided more data about thrust-fault location, surface ruptures and dam-age potential. Evidence that folds associated with hid-den thrust faults grew during earthquakes came in 1983 at Coalinga and in 1987 at Whittier Narrows. The earthquake potential of these elusive faults was fully realized. Surveys taken before and after these events

provided data needed to measure the surface deforma-tion that resulted.

Even though the surface may rupture in only the largest thrust-fault earthquakes, measurable changes in surface expression may turn out to be just as valu-able at pinpointing earthquake sources as the linear topographic features that identify strike-slip faults.

The Transverse Ranges
An extensive band of active reverse and thrust faults is found in the Transverse Mountain Ranges along the northern side of the Los Angeles Basin and under the San Gabriel and San Fernando Valleys.

The Transverse Ranges are very unusual in that they run east-west, rather than north-south like most other mountain ranges in the United States. Starting in the west at Point Conception and moving eastward, major pieces of the Transverse Ranges are the Santa Ynez range, and the Santa Susana, Santa Monica, San Gabriel, and San Bernardino Mountains.

These mountain ranges owe their existence to the squeezing, bending and uplifting of rocks during movements along the curved portion of the San Andreas fault system between Tejon Pass (Interstate 5) and San Gorgonio Pass (Interstate 10). Instead of the Pacific and North American plates sliding by each

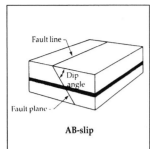

Fault line

Dip angle

Fault plane

AB-slip

Right lateral strike-slip faulting

Left lateral strike-slip faulting

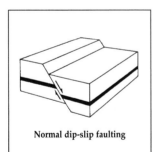

Normal dip-slip faulting

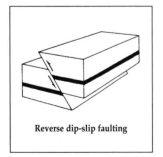

Reverse dip-slip faulting

Very few fault planes are truly vertical; the dip angle varies considerably among major faults. The most common movements on California faults are right-lateral strike-slip or reverse dip-slip.

TYPES OF FAULTS

Faults are not simple structures. Very few can be described in simple terms and they have an irritating habit of changing character at different points along their length, and at different depths. In the most general terms, there are two basic types:

Strike-slip faults are characterized by essentially horizontal slipping along vertical or near-vertical planes. The horizontal movement may be either right-lateral or left-lateral. The San Andreas fault is a right-lateral, strike-slip fault. If you stand on one side of the fault and look across it, the movement of the opposite side is always to the right. Most northwest-trending faults in the San Andreas system are characterized by this same right-lateral movement. A few other California strike-slip faults with different trend lines, including the Garlock, are left-lateral.

The 1989 Loma Prieta quake cast some doubts on whether the San Andreas fault is as vertical as originally thought. Aftershock patterns defined a dipping plane that would not coincide with the San Andreas if extended to the surface. It could be that the fault includes a dip component at some depth below the surface, or the quake originated on an unknown, unmapped branch.

Despite all the recent attention to thrust-fault movement generated by recent Southern California quakes, strike-slip is still the dominant fault motion in California, and the branches of the San Andreas System will continue to pose the greatest earthquake threat in the future.

Dip-slip faults are characterized by a dominant component of vertical slip along dipping or angled fault planes; these planes are not exactly vertical, but are more like steep ramps with one rock formation overhanging the other. The upper rock formation is called the *hanging-wall block* and the rock below the fracture is called the *foot-wall block.* There are three variants of dip-slip faults:

1. Normal faults, where the hanging-wall block slips downward relative to the foot-wall block.
2. Reverse faults, where the hanging-wall block moves upward relative to the foot-wall block.
3. Thrust faults, which are reverse faults with shallow dips.

In thrust-faulting, it is typical for the break to start at the bottom and move upward. Unfortunately, this terminology often becomes confused, with the term "thrust" used to describe any dip-slip fault in Southern California, regardless of the dip angle. Very often, "reverse" is a more accurate term.

Sometimes, the dip of the fault changes close to the surface; the deeper part of the San Fernando fault that caused the 1971 quake has a steep dip, and is called a *reverse fault,* which is consistent with the entire Sierra Madre fault zone. However, the near-surface plane where the surface ruptured in this particular quake was much shallower and can be labeled as a *thrust fault.* The thrusting caused the hanging wall, the upper San Gabriel Mountain block, to move upward and westward relative to the foot wall, the lower San Fernando Valley block.

The degree of dip can also change along the length of the fault. At its western, exposed end, the Oak Ridge fault is a reverse fault with a dip of 70 degrees. Farther east, where the 1994 Northridge earthquake is thought to have originated, the fault plane is much shallower and can be described as a thrust fault. It could be that these two sections are not continuous.

The Cleveland Hill fault responsible for the August 1, 1975, Oroville earthquake (M5.7) is a normal dip-slip fault. The 1983 Coalinga and 1987 Whittier Narrows quakes occurred on thrust faults with a dip of about 25 degrees. The 1952 Kern County and 1989 Loma Prieta earthquakes were unusual in that they were caused by oblique movements that included almost equal amounts of strike-slip and reverse-slip components. Oblique-slip by itself is not unusual, but equal amounts of both components is rarely observed.

Some reverse faults equal in length to strike-slip faults can generate bigger earthquakes, because their shallow angles can have wider rupture surfaces. Also, it takes more energy to push rock up rather than sideways. As a result, a 12-mile-long fault has the capacity to produce a maximum earthquake of about M6.0 if it is strike-slip and about M6.7 if it is a thrust fault.

Instrumental readings of recent Southern California quakes indicate that reverse- and thrust-fault movements may also produce stronger shaking than quakes of similar size on strike-slip faults. But more data is needed from large strike-slip quakes to validate this theory.

The 1987 Whittier Narrows earthquake ended an unusually quiet seismic period in southern California. It provided important data on faults in the Transverse Mountain Ranges.

Size of a fault, magnitude of an earthquake and amount of damage resulting from that quake are not always directly relational. In 1925, a quake of only M6.3, originating on an unknown minor fault in the Santa Barbara channel, laid waste to the coastal communities. Arlington Hotel (left) was only one of several substantial buildings that sustained major damage and alerted public officials to the need for better design and construction standards.

other, as is the case in Northern California and in deepest Southern California, they crunch against each other along the great bend. The Pacific Plate is squeezed and compressed, and strain builds up in all directions. Relief comes through folding, uplift and reverse faulting in addition to the strike-slip faulting typical of the San Andreas system.

The 1987 Whittier Narrows quake (see page 111) drew attention to one of the dip-slip faults associated with the Transverse Ranges, the Elysian Park Fold and Thrust Belt that extends from the Santa Monica Mountains along the Malibu coast, through downtown Los Angeles, and into Orange County in the southeast. The 1971 San Fernando quake occurred on the San Fernando branch of the Sierra Madre fault zone that extends along the base of the San Gabriel Mountains from San Fernando to a junction with the San Jacinto fault near San Bernardino. The 1994 Northridge quake is thought to have originated on a previously unrecognized extension of the Oak Ridge fault that extends from Ventura to the Santa Clarita River Valley.

Other named faults in this set include the Compton-Los Alamitos thrust fault, identified from the Baldwin Hills area to Los Alamitos; the Whittier fault, in the eastern Los Angeles basin; the Santa Monica and Hollywood faults that form the northern edge of the basin; and the Torrance-Wilmington Fold and Thrust Belt that extends 40 miles from offshore Newport Beach, across the Palos Verdes Peninsula and into Santa Monica Bay.

Northern California Thrust Faults

In Northern California, the San Andreas fault makes another bend at Black Mountain in the Santa Cruz Mountains (near the epicenter of the 1989 earthquake). This change in direction has given rise to another cluster of reverse and thrust faults under the Santa Clara valley from Los Gatos to Los Altos Hills. Another band lies off the San Mateo County coast. Compression along this bend, and the reverse thrusting that typifies earthquakes originating here, caused the rapid uplift of the coastal mountains.

Another thrust-fault zone is found on the eastern slope of the Berkeley Hills north of Hayward, thought to be part of the Hayward fault zone (see page 43). The northernmost significant cluster is associated with the Cascadia Subduction Zone on the north coast (see page 26).

The San Andreas Fault

The most seismically active and topographically conspicuous fault in California is the San Andreas. Movements along this tectonic boundary over the last three-million years have affected an area from Cape

Movements along Garlock Fault upended and deformed rocks that form south end of the Slate Range. Flat, undisturbed surface at right is alluvial outwash from the mountains. Brown Valley and southern tip of the Panamint Valley are in background. G. I. Smith photo.

Mendocino to the Salton Sea, and from offshore areas in the Pacific Ocean to the Great Central Valley and Mojave Desert. It caused two of the great earthquakes in California's history—1857 and 1906—plus a number of others that excited public interest.

Structure of The San Andeas Fault

What is generally called *The San Andreas fault* consists of several structures—an overall system, zones within the system, individual faults within the zones and separate strands with their own names.

The San Andreas fault system is large and complex. It is a network of interwoven, roughly parallel branches that converge, separate and interact with each other. Its length extends more than 835 miles from Cape Mendocino to the Mexican border.

The system is not of a single age, and includes the remnants of ancient faults that have been quiet for countless millennia, as well as newly active strands. This discontinuous movement has given rise to a confused surface appearance consisting of heavily eroded features, plus the fresher results of movements of the past few-thousand years.

Within the San Andreas fault system a number of subparallel major fault zones have similar characteristics, including the main line of the San Andreas itself, plus several others large enough to warrant names of

their own, including Hayward, Calaveras, Imperial, Elsinore and San Jacinto.

The San Andreas fault zone ranges in width from less than a hundred yards to several miles, and extends to depths of at least 15 miles and probably as much as 60 miles, to the bottom edge of the lithosphere. In most areas, it is made up of any number of sub-parallel fractures. The zone is not smooth or straight. Tectonic plates on either side have irregular shapes, and the fault conforms.

The line of most recent activity within the zone is quite narrow, and sometimes can be recognized as a single break between different rock types; this is what is most commonly called "the" San Andreas fault.

Topography of the San Andreas Fault

Over its length, the San Andreas fault zone is generally revealed as a linear trough or shallow valley of variable width that cuts through all types of topography—mountains, deserts, flat plains—that is often described as a rift valley. This trough results both from surface effects of recent fault movements, and from erosion in the crushand broken rocks. While the rock formations on either side remain solid, the rubble caused by the shearing action along the fault is easily weathered and eroded. It is washed away by rain and rivers that tend to push their courses through the soft

BAJA CALIFORNIA

Outside of California, the most striking example of accumulated horizontal displacement concerns the origin of Baja California and the gulf separating it from the Mexican mainland.

Southeast of Baja, the straight coastline of the Mexican mainland is broken by an abrupt southwestern swing of some 100 miles near Jalisco. The shape of this indentation roughly approximates the shape of the southern tip of the Baja peninsula. Geologic features suggest Baja was once attached to this part of the mainland. Horizontal movements along the San Andreas Fault caused the peninsula to break away and move northwest, thereby forming the unusual deep-water gap of the Gulf of California.

Total horizontal movement required for this shift is only 250 miles, certainly reasonable in light of observable movements along other parts of the fault. And the gulf is being widened at the rate of about two inches a year—the same rate that characterizes movement along the fault in California.

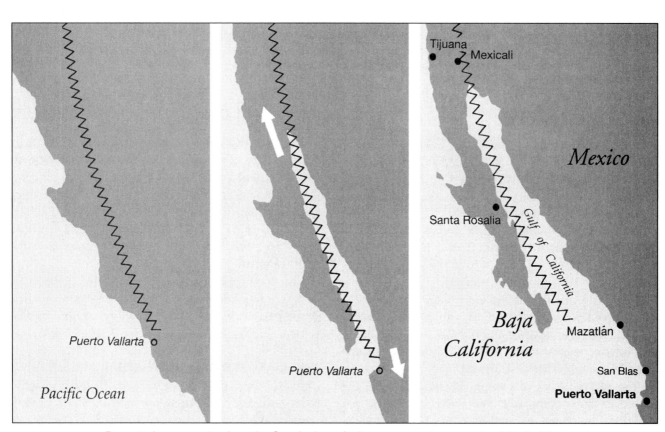

Repeated movements along the San Andreas fault zone caused an oversize "slice" of the Mexican mainland to break away and move northwest. Each new right-lateral movement added to the separation, until the new peninsula assumed its present position. Even today, many of Mexico's earthquakes originate in the deep gulf trench.

While the San Andreas fault receives most of the publicity, other, lesser-known faults have been responsible for many significant earthquakes in this century and last. Downtown Tehachapi sustained major damage in the 1952 Kern County earthquake. It was important not only for the test it provided to design and construction standards, but also in helping to improve scientific understanding of hidden thrust faults (see page 27). In downtown areas, older, unreinforced buildings that characterized pre-1933 construction were badly damaged. More modern buildings such as the two-story reinforced concrete structure in the background held up very well. Wide World Photos.

Long surface ruptures occur only in major earthquakes, and not always then. The 1906 San Francisco quake tore the earth for more than 250 miles. Greatest displacement was in Marin County. The 1857 Tejon Pass quake caused a 200-mile surface break. These ruptures are not be confused with secondary cracking and slumping, which is quite common in even moderate quakes (see page 78). G. K. Gilbert photo.

Fault movements along east side of the Sierra Nevada created a magnificent fault escarpment. Active branches of the fault system lie at the base of the Alabama Hills (foreground) and were responsible for the great 1872 Owens Valley earthquake (see page 91). Glenn M. Christiansen photo.

Eroded escarpments are among the most easily recognized features along the San Andreas Fault. This rounded, elongate hillock, with the most active fault trace on the steep side, is in Carrizo Plain.

Unusual double-scarp formation in Carrizo Plain, with depressed block or graben in between, indicates two lines of recent activity. The right escarpment is much lower than the left.

THE SIERRA NEVADA

The most spectacular example of accumulated vertical movement along a California fault is the eastern escarpment of the Sierra Nevada, a great fault block that slowly raised and tilted westward over several-million years. The steep eastern face clearly marks the line of the Owens Valley Fault. (see photo at left)

This scarp is highest and most clearly defined between Big Pine and Olancha, at the southern end of Owens Valley. There the face of the range is not broken by any foothills. Ridge spurs truncated by the faulting may be seen south of Owens Lake and southwest of Independence.

West of Independence, the contour of the Sierra scarp changes, with the addition of foothills that have not been depressed as far as Owens Valley and have not been lifted as far as the escarpment. But as far north as Birch Mountain, the eastern face of the range presents unmistakable proof of its development by repeated dislocations along the fault zone.

Owens Valley itself is a long, narrow block that has been steadily sinking relative to the mountains to the west that have been tilting upward.

Even though this fault system was responsible for the great Owens Valley quake of 1872, most movements here barely rate a mention in the popular media, because it is too far from major population centers to create much notice.

An escarpment caused by vertical movements on this fault, including the 1872 earthquake, can be seen within a mile of Lone Pine, on the former channel of Lone Pine Creek at the end of the Whitney Portal Highway west out of town.

deposits. The zone's edges are sometimes indefinite because many old lines of activity are now hidden under recent gravel deposits or alluvium, and because of landslides that cover several miles at a stretch.

While the very large, eroded escarpments that stand thousands of feet high along the edges of faults are the result of millions of years of movements over a wide zone, most of the lesser details you will find are along the line of most recent activity within the zone. Even though this activity may have occurred hundreds or thousands of years ago, it is still "recent" in geologic terms. In most cases, the features are the result of several huge earthquakes spread over any number of centuries. Many fault movements are required to create a new ridge or shift a hillslope to block drainage and create a sag pond.

It is true that very recent large earthquakes such as those of 1906 and 1857 "freshened" some features of the San Andreas Fault and in some cases created new low escarpments and sag areas that can still be seen today. These are rare, and it is very seldom that any significant feature can be assigned to a single movement.

Novice fault explorers may have difficulty identifying fault features; it becomes easier with more exploration. In some cases, shape recognition is the key recognition factor; elsewhere, it is color change where rocks of one kind on one side of the fault plane abut different rocks of another color on the other side. It is often best to do your exploration in either early morning or late afternoon when low light and long shadows cause stretches of the fault to stand out like a dark river through the rounded hills.

The three most common fault features are escarpments, offset streams and sag ponds:

Escarpments, or *"scarps,"* are steep cliffs or ridges formed by surface ruptures. They can be created by either vertical or horizontal movement. In an area of mixed high and low relief, a horizontal fault movement may break open a hill or ridge and expose a steep interior face along the line of rupture. Only the face of the scarp is steep and aligned along the fault—other nearby slopes will have a much more gradual slope. Scarps that have their steep face toward the mountains are better preserved because erosion tends to emphasize them. There are hundreds along the San Andreas fault, ranging in height from a few feet to a mile or more. In some instances, they are the only evidence of recent rupture along the San Andreas fault.

The *offset* in the routes of rivers and streams that cross the fault at right angles offers one of the best ways to determine the line of most recent activity. Because displacement is accumulated slowly by repeated movement, streams tend to hold onto old channels, even though they become increasingly offset.

EARLY RECOGNITION

The first notion that a huge fault cut through California came in 1893, when geologist Andrew Lawson took a steamer trip from San Diego to San Francisco, stopping to examine the coastal topography at several places. He noted that San Benito, Santa Clara, and the San Francisco Bay valleys were remarkably linear, and that the general uplift of the continental margin was tilted and marked by forces that "may yet be active."

The San Andreas fault received its name two years later, when Lawson pointed out that the fault features were best exposed and typified by the straight valley on the San Francisco peninsula that was occupied in part by San Andreas Lake.

The image of San Andreas fault is so dominant in the minds of both Californians and observers around the world that it is often mistakenly blamed for *all* the state's earthquake destruction. But even with this conspicuous international image, the fault's topographic expressions are often unrecognized or misinterpreted by residents and visitors.

Nineteenth-century settlers who unexpectedly found a narrow valley and—of all things—a marshy pond high in the hot Coast Range foothills may not have considered cause and effect, but they quickly dammed the pond and drove their stock to the welcome water.

In the post World War II housing boom, developers eyed with envy the high bluffs that jutted up at the edges of flat valleys, but rarely asked why these unusual ridges were juxtaposed with lower terrain.

Modern-day Southern Californians who enjoy their high mountains and flat deserts within minutes of each other probably never consider just how this could happen, nor do they relate their existence with the sharp midnight shudder that activates the car alarm and sets the neighborhood dogs to barking.

The early morning or late afternoon air traveler between San Francisco and Los Angeles may be fascinated by the giant shadowy scar that stands out in the arid stretch of the central Coast Range, but he is likely to dismiss it as a trick of the weather.

This lack of public recognition does not extend to the scientific community. Because of its immense size and geologic importance, the San Andreas fault has been (and continues to be) the subject of intense geologic study ever since its existence was first recognized.

Passengers flying between the San Francisco Bay area and southern California can be startled by their first view of the straight line of the San Andreas fault in Carrizo Plain. J. R. Balsley photo.

After a few centuries, the stream bed assumes a curved shape that is unique to fault topography. Carrizo Plain is one of the best places in the world to see offset streams—almost all the drainage lines show displacement. More good examples can be seen at Pt. Reyes, south of Cholame, near Valyermo, and at most other sections of the fault where movement has been consistent and where small stream beds cross the fault rather than flow along it.

Sag ponds are enclosed, undrained areas within the fault zone. They are created by multiple fracturing, uplifting and tilting of the earth so all drainage avenues are cut off. The undrained reservoirs thus formed become basins for runoff from surrounding high ground. Sag ponds are almost as common as scarps along the San Andreas fault. They show up at all elevations and in all types of terrain; many have been modified into small reservoirs or watering holes for livestock. Among the most conspicuous are the Elizabeth Lake basin and Lost Lake at Cajon Pass.

Several other features characterize the fault zone:

Saddles are formed where the fault cuts across a steep slope or ridge top, and the resulting band of crushed rock is eroded into a shallow swale that interrupts the normal ridge contours. Good examples of this feature are in Marin County, on the slopes west of Gorman, and at Big Pines Summit.

Offset streams, as in Carrizo Plain (left), give geologists a good indication of the amount of movement along fault segments. Only a few feet—or even inches—of offset may occur in a single quake, so the stream bed adjusts itself without being blocked completely. Characteristic S-shape develops as the result of many separate quakes. At ground level (right), amount of offset can be measured precisely and matched with age of the rocks and alluvium to determine the slip rate. This stream bed has offset about 45 feet during the last 250-300 years. Truncated hills on the left side of the photo are clear examples of how fault cuts a straight line across and through topographic features. U. S. Geological Survey photos.

Sunken blocks (or grabens) develop between two parallel, active branches of a fault that either push down the area between them, or leave it behind as they rise as mountains on either side. Once the basic structure is established, then erosion adds its work to accent and emphasize the sunken block. Both the Cholame and Imperial valleys are this type of broad flat valley with steep slopes on either side.

The multiple fracturing that goes on within a fault zone often causes a pattern of alternating elevated and depressed crustal blocks that are expressed by long, narrow ridges separated by deep troughs or gullies. This type of development can also be created or emphasized by differential erosion. Crystal Springs and San Andreas Lakes are located in an area of apparent uplift and depression actually caused by horizontal fault movement that juxtaposes high topography against low.

Where mountain ranges are bounded by faults, the slopes that are in direct contact with a fault tend to be very steep, without any foothills. The eastern face of the Gabilan range south of Hollister, the southern slopes of the San Bernardino Mountains, and the San Jacinto Mountains near Soboba Hot Springs illustrate this phenomenon.

Side-hill ridges are the result of surface rupture and erosion. When an earthquake breaks the surface along

COMPLEXITY

It turns out that the San Andreas fault system is most complex in the areas of greatest population density. The situation under and around the metropolitan San Francisco Bay Area is described on page 126. In Southern California, more than 12-million people live in the Los Angeles, San Fernando, San Gabriel and San Bernardino basins. North of this highly developed area, the San Andreas fault is marked by a great bend thought to be at least partially responsible for the development of an extremely complex set of active faults with high potential for future quakes (see page 28).

East of San Diego, the San Andreas system is so wide that almost the entire width of the state falls under the spell of this great system. Major branches include the Newport-Inglewood and Rose Canyon faults on the coast; the Elsinore, San Jacinto, Coyote Creek, Superstition Hills, and Imperial fault zones farther inland; and the main branch of San Andreas fault east of the Salton Sea.

Other parallel faults located offshore add additional width to the overall system. In cross section, this southernmost segment resembles an inclined block. It is highest along the northern San Andreas fault in the San Gabriel Mountains and lowest on the floor of the Catalina Basin, a downhill slope that drops more than 8,000 feet. This tilt is the result of regional uplifts and downward movements on a combination of strike-slip and dip-slip faults.

HOW FAR, HOW FAST?

Slip rates, or rates of movement between the blocks of rock on opposite sides of the San Andreas fault, vary in different sections, from 3/4 inch to almost two inches per year (see page 25). The best measurements available indicate that the aggregate movement for the last 15-20 million years has averaged 15 to 20 feet per century, for a total horizontal displacement of at least 350 miles. If this trend continues for several million more years, the area we know as Los Angeles—on the Pacific Plate west of the San Andreas fault—could someday be at the same latitude as Sacramento, located on the North American plate.

Because of this horizontal movement, only rarely do old rock types on opposite sides of the San Andreas fault match each other. To substantiate the rate of movement, geologists locate a distinctive rock formation on one side of the fault, then find that same formation on the other side and measure the displacement. By comparing the displacement with the age of the rock, the minimum amount of movement during the intervening time span can be estimated.

This is more difficult than it sounds, because matching rocks on both sides of the fault are difficult to find. The same fault movements that cause the displacement may also uplift the formations to where erosion can wear them away, or depress them to where younger layers of gravel and rock can bury them from sight. Then, too, positive identification of what appear to be similar rock formations can be difficult.

The map at right indicates three noteworthy match-ups:

1. Rocks west of the fault between Point Arena and Bodega Head match rocks in the Eagle Rest Peak area in the San Emigdio Mountains, just east of the fault, an offset of 350 miles in less than 150-million years.

2. Rocks of Pinnacles Volcanic Formation west of the fault match the Neenach Volcanic Formation, northeast of the fault in the Mojave Desert, about 12 miles south of the San Andreas-Garlock fault intersection, an offset of almost 200 miles in less than 50-million years.

3. Staggered relationships of gravel beds west of the fault in the Logan area and in the Temblor Mountains near Gold Hill indicate displacement of about 10 miles in less than one-million years.

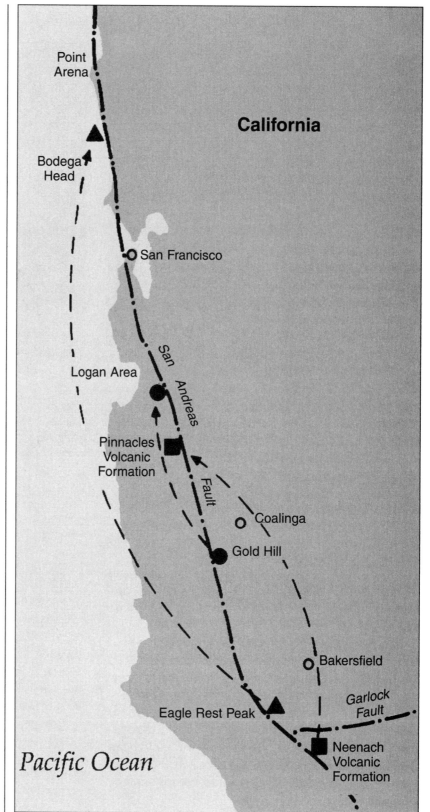

Sag ponds are other commonly found fault features. Many, such as the dry basin in Carrizo Plain (left) serve as natural drainage basins and are dry much of the year. Others (right) have been dammed to form artificial reservoirs in the dry coastal foothills.

the side of a ridge, the line of weakness invites erosion. The downhill side of the break is still resistant, and it stands firm while the crushed rocks along the fault are worn away. Eventually, the edge of the downhill slope juts above grade and forms a secondary ridge that is an erosional feature and has nothing to do with normal mountain building. Examples can be found on the Earthquake Trail at Los Trancos Preserve and along Cienega Road south of Hollister.

Slice ridges can be created in one of two ways. Most often, rock is squeezed between two parallel faults and forced upward into a hogback or long slender ridge. These are quite common; the rift valley west of Palmdale contains a very prominent example. Sometimes, a "slice" of rock or mountain slope breaks away from its parent mass and begins to move alone within the fault zone. A large slice ridge of this latter type can be seen east of Cienega Road south of Hollister.

For much of its course, the San Andreas fault marks the dividing line between radically different rock types. In some areas, only rock hounds will be able to differentiate between the various deposits along the fault; but everyone can see the differences in color and rock patterns at Devil's Punchbowl, in Whitewater Canyon and at Mill Creek north of Beaumont.

When two hard faces along a fault plane rub togeth-er during an earthquake, they crush and grind rocks between them. The rocks are both physically and chemically altered until many of the minerals turn into a clay-like impermeable substance, most often black in color, called *gouge*. Fault zones thereby acquire a buffer of this crushed rock that may be only as wide as a pencil in a small fault, or hundreds of feet wide in an active and complex fault zone such as the San Andreas.

When subterranean water channels and gravel beds are disrupted by fault movements, or run into a line of gouge, water backs up on the uphill side of the fault. If the impounded ground water has enough pressure behind it to force a path to the surface, a spring or small lake is formed. If the water doesn't find its way to the surface, the water table may be raised high enough to support an uncommon concentration of vegetation. In Southern California's desert areas, lines of impounded ground water often mark the fault trace across sand and rock. In Whitewater Canyon and on the southern extension of Big Rock Creek, dense lines of vegetation spring from otherwise barren flat lands. In Seven Palms Valley, a wide strip of palms and brush cuts through the hot desert floor. North of Indio, a long series of oases and scattered palms rests on the fault.

Hot springs are common along the San Andreas, the San Jacinto and other major faults in Southern California. Many are commercially developed into

This offset fence typified the large horizontal movements in Marin County caused by the 1906 earthquake. The fence has been recreated along the Earthquake Trail at Pt. Reyes National Seashore. G.R. Gilbert Photo.

popular health and resort areas. The heat probably is caused by friction of the rocks sliding past one another.

The California Coast Ranges are known for their landslides, and one contributing factor is the San Andreas Fault. The fault causes landslides in two ways. First, the steep mountain slopes associated with fault-controlled ranges are ideal ramps for landslides. Second, the multiple fractures that occur within the fault zone shatter and weaken the rocks so they are ready for a landslide the first time they become overloaded with water.

Repeated fracturing of rocks along the steep northern face of the San Gabriel Mountains aided in setting the scene for the historic 1941 mudflow at Wrightwood. The eastern slope of Slack Canyon north of Parkfield is one continuous landslide area owing to the proximity of the fault and to the rock types in the fault zone. And at Mussel Rock south of San Francisco, where the San Andreas Fault emerges from the sea onto land, all traces of the fault line are lost in a giant landslide area.

Exploring the San Andreas Fault

Most of the time, the fault is recognizable by a dis-continuous chain of features; in a few areas, it disappears in dense forests or sandy deserts. The 12 numbered locations on the map are easiest to find and explore.

The Northern Section

The San Andreas fault's northernmost extension is at Cape Mendocino, site of the triple junction where three tectonic plates meet (see page 26). The location is identified by a marker at A Way County Park in Petrolia.

The fault itself is first clearly visible on land near Point Arena; the site is marked with an informational sign at the parking area at the mouth of Alder Creek. Just north of Manchester, Crispin Road crosses sag ponds that mark the site of the 1906 rupture.

Southward, the fault zone parallels the coast along the routes of the Garcia and Gualala rivers. Fort Ross Road, across from the entrance to Fort Ross State Park, crosses two traces of the 1906 quake within a mile of State Highway 1. The rupture line is marked by a series of alternating trenches and low ridges, sag ponds and small scarps.

At this point, the fault disappears underwater again, re-emerging as a broad swath that separates Bodega

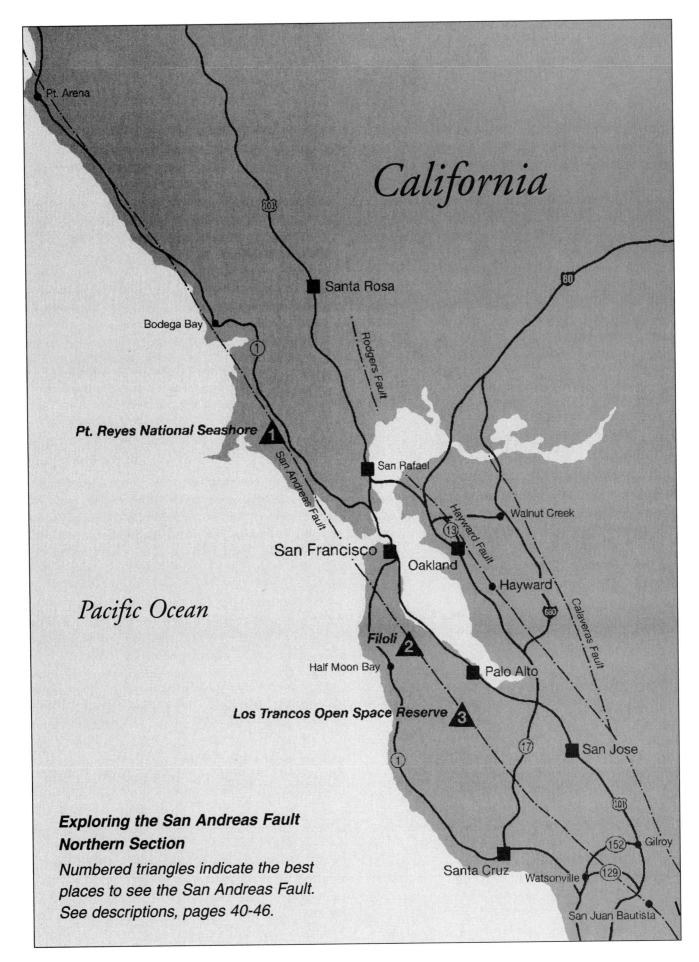

California

Pt. Arena

Santa Rosa

Bodega Bay

Rodgers Fault

Pt. Reyes National Seashore 1

San Rafael

San Andreas Fault

Walnut Creek

Hayward Fault

13

Pacific Ocean

San Francisco

Oakland

Hayward

680

Calaveras Fault

Filoli 2

Half Moon Bay

Palo Alto

Los Trancos Open Space Reserve 3

17

1

San Jose

101

**Exploring the San Andreas Fault
Northern Section**

*Numbered triangles indicate the best
places to see the San Andreas Fault.
See descriptions, pages 40-46.*

152 Gilroy

129

Santa Cruz   Watsonville

San Juan Bautista

Garcia Creek follows the San Andreas fault south of Point Arena (Pacific Ocean in the background). The most active trace within the fault zone is on the left side of the creek bed. Robert E. Wallace photo.

The valley of the San Andreas fault crosses Bodega Head (visible in the background) and then divides Pt. Reyes Peninsula on the left from the Marin County mainland. Photo by Clyde Sunderland Aerial Photographs.

Head and the mainland, and divides Point Reyes Peninsula and the Marin County mainland. Both Tomales Bay and Bolinas Lagoon are fault-controlled features. On Sir Francis Drake Boulevard, just east of the junction with Bear Valley Road, is the site of the maximum lateral displacement in the 1906 earthquake—18 feet.

1. POINT REYES NATIONAL SEASHORE. The Park Headquarters is on the site of the Skinner Ranch where the 1906 quake caused horizontal displacements of 14 to 16 feet in a fence, path and cow barn. A paved, self-guided Earthquake Trail circles out into the fault zone, with frequent markers to point out fault features and explain fault mechanics. A line of blue posts marks the line of rupture of the 1906 quake and an offset fence illustrates the horizontal movement. A display points out different rock types on opposite sides of the fault. One marker presents both sides of the story of a cow that might have fallen into a fissure.

From Olema to Bolinas Lagoon, the fault is just west of State Highway 1. It is revealed by a series of low ridges and sag ponds. Fault movements here have jumbled the landscape to such an extent that Olema Creek and Pine Gulch Creek, a few hundred feet apart, flow in opposite directions.

South of Bolinas, the fault lies under the Gulf of the Farallones, west of the Golden Gate Bridge. It emerges on land again at Mussel Rock, about three miles south of San Francisco, and extends southward on the east side of Interstate 280. It is easy to trace the fault zone here, because much of it is drowned under Upper and Lower Crystal Springs Lakes. These reservoirs, along with San Andreas Lake, hold San Francisco's water supply.

San Andreas Dam, at the southern end of San Andreas Lake, was built in the 1860s and then raised in height in 1875 and 1928. Even though the dam was displaced horizontally about nine feet by the 1906 earthquake, it did not fail because the break was confined to a bedrock ridge that forms the eastern abutment of the dam. The Lower Crystal Springs Dam was constructed in 1887-1890 as one of the largest concrete dams in the world at the time. The 1906 earthquake ruptured the reservoir floor a thousand feet west of the dam but did not cause the slightest crack in the concrete—a tribute to the engineers.

2. FILOLI. The historic and beautiful house and gardens developed by Mr. and Mrs. William Bourn in the early 1900s and administered as a property of the National Trust For Historic Preservation, lies right in the San Andreas fault zone. The entrance is on Canada Road in Woodside, just west of Interstate 280. Nature hikes led by docents are available every morning except Sunday. Fault features include an escarpment, sag ponds, and

THE HAYWARD FAULT

The Hayward fault runs along the eastern edge of San Francisco Bay, and is an active branch of the San Andreas fault system. Earthquakes originating here have had a significant impact on the area's geography. Considered one of the faults most likely to generate another large quake sometime during the next few decades, it has been (and continues to be) the subject of intense scrutiny.

The northern terminus is under San Pablo Bay, a short right step away from the southern end of the Rodgers Creek fault. It is traceable as far south as the Niles area, where it makes another short step along the short Mission fault to merge with the Calaveras fault zone near Calaveras Reservoir. Fault features are conspicuous along most of the route.

In the El Cerrito-Richmond area, the line of faulting is marked by a series of shallow depressions and a small valley. On the University of California campus, Strawberry Creek has been offset by almost a quarter of a mile. The fault passes directly under Memorial Stadium (about on the west sideline of the football field). Offsets caused by slow creep can be seen in the wall above Gate 8, and underneath the seats inside the stadium.

The fault is clearly defined as it passes just southwest of the interchange of State Highways 13 and 24, west of the Caldecott Tunnel in the Oakland and Berkeley Hills. Lake Temescal is an ancient sag pond that was dammed and enlarged to create the present reservoir. The fault trace is just a few feet from the eastern edge of the dam. Temescal Creek is significantly offset as it flows out of the hills and into the lake.

To the south, the fault follows the long linear valley through the Oakland Hills that is the route of State Highway 13. Offset streams are common here. In San Leandro, the fault runs along the base of a low hill at the back of Fairmont Hospital. Some of the hospital's original buildings had to be torn down because of their location on top of the fault. In the city of Hayward, evidence of slow creep is most clearly seen in street cracking, curb offsets and building damage in the downtown area bounded by Mission Boulevard and Main Street, especially on A and D Streets.

A conspicuously offset dry stream bed north of Mission Boulevard on the steep hill at the end of MacDonald Way marks the fault trace in Union City. South of the Masonic Home, the fault zone is 15-30 feet wide where a stream offset indicates right-lateral movement of more than 150 feet.

Fences at the Shinn Street Railroad Station in Fremont have distinct offsets that resulted from long-term creep of about an inch a year. The Fremont BART station parking lot partially covers a large sag pond; to the south, the marshy area is confined by two escarpments marking active traces of the fault.

In Fremont Central Park, the City Hall sits atop an elevated rise between two branches of the Hayward fault. There are offset curbs on Sailway Drive and on the south end of the Senior Center parking lot, and a series of cracks in the asphalt path from the old library building to the lake. Just south of the park, pipes carrying water from Hetch Hetchy reservoir in the Sierra Nevada to reservoirs on the San Francisco peninsula are bent in a right-lateral direction due to fault creep.

Compression between the merging Hayward and Calaveras fault zones has created the highest hills on the east side of San Francisco Bay, from Monument Peak to Mission Peak. Anderson, Coyote and San Felipe Lakes all occupy valleys within the combined fault zone.

Hayward fault runs along the University of California's Memorial Stadium. The offset totals almost five inches since the stadium was built in the 1930s, and is most evident looking upward in front of Gate 8. Photo courtesy University of California EERC Library.

The mountainous area from Old Alpine Road (left) south toward the Salinas area (right) was marked by large sections of slumping and dislocations in the flatlands. This experience was repeated in the 1989 earthquake.

The 1906 quake created an eight-foot offset in this fence near Filoli. California Division of Mines and Geology photo.

mismatched rocks on opposite sides of the fault. (For information on tours, reservations and fees, phone 415-364-2880.)

3. Los Trancos Open Space Preserve. Administered by the Midpeninsula Regional Open Space District, this wooded area offers another self-guided tour along the San Andreas fault. The entrance is on Page Mill Road, about seven miles west of Interstate 280, on the north side of the road opposite the Montebello Open Space Preserve. The trail is 0.6 mile long and has 13 marked stations identifying fault features; trail brochures are available at the trailhead. Striped markers indicate the fault, a reconstructed fence shows horizontal movement, and there are a number of sag ponds, trees that were damaged in the 1906 earthquake, springs created by the damming action of fault movements and some long-range views of the fault valley to the north.

South of Page Mill Road, the fault follows the canyon of Stevens Creek. You can either hike the area within the Montebello Preserve or stop at one of the pullouts along Skyline Boulevard for views across the fault valley.

State Highway 17 crosses the fault about 1. 5 miles north of Summit Road. To the south, Summit Road and Highland Way follow a fault valley that sustained

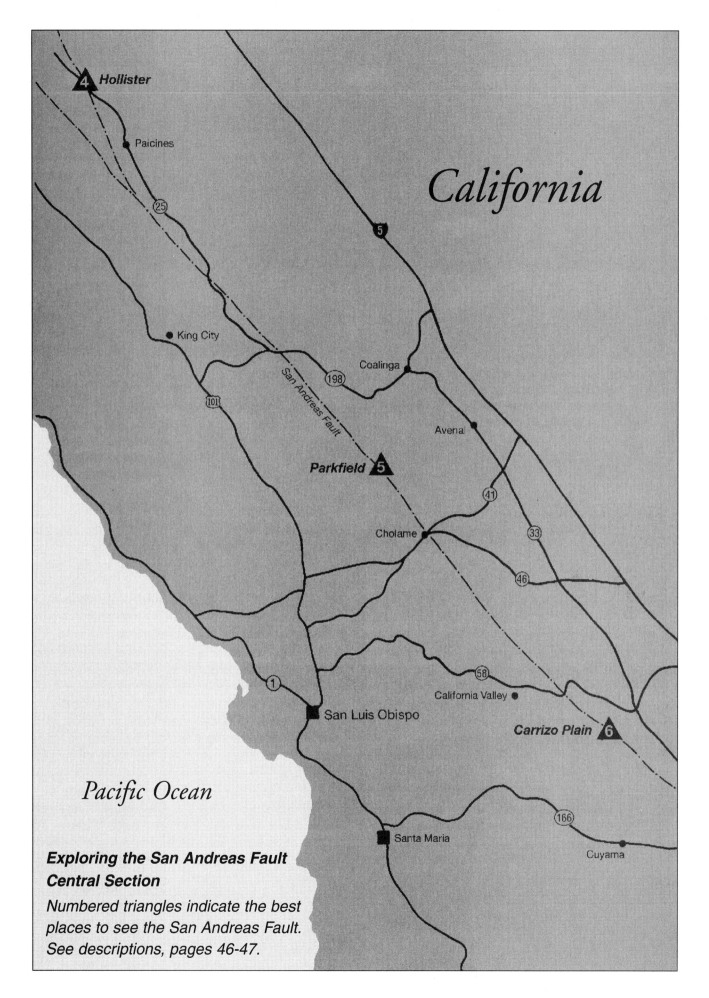

California

Hollister

Paicines

25

5

King City

198   Coalinga

101

San Andreas Fault

Avenal

Parkfield 5

41

Cholame

33

46

1

58

California Valley

San Luis Obispo

Carrizo Plain 6

Pacific Ocean

166

Santa Maria

Cuyama

Exploring the San Andreas Fault Central Section

Numbered triangles indicate the best places to see the San Andreas Fault. See descriptions, pages 46-47.

Slow creep at a winery south of Hollister has offset drainage channels and damaged interior walls. Creep continues on an intermittent basis, with periods of quiet and "instant" creep, depending on other seismic activity on the San Andreas and Hayward faults.

One steep escarpment is visible on Coalinga road (most recent activity has been along the steep eastern side). A similar scarp is visible a few miles north in Little Rabbit Valley.

extensive ground slumping and landsliding in both the 1906 and 1989 earthquakes. The Summit Road-Morrell Road intersection was the location of very unusual left-lateral movements in both quakes. Fault features are most noticeable both north and south of the Burrell Forest Fire Station on Highland Road, and then again farther south at the intersection of Hazel Dell Road and Mt. Madonna Road, where a sag area lies west of the road and a gentle valley stretches out to the north.

A scarp on an ancient trace of the San Andreas fault passes through the grounds of Mission San Juan Bautista and forms the foundation for the grandstand at the rodeo grounds. The tiers of grandstand seats fit comfortably on the scarp incline and the Mission itself is on the highest ground, the top of the escarpment.

This is the southernmost area where the ground ruptured in 1906, and it is the northernmost point where slow creep is visible along the fault.

The Central Section

4. HOLLISTER. While not on the main San Andreas fault, this is one of the most active seismic areas in the state. The Calaveras fault passes through the center of town. Frequent small quakes and slow creep within this zone are accepted as a normal part of life (the 1989 Loma Prieta earthquake triggered cracks in a field south of 7th Street). Cienega Valley Winery, on Cienega Road

about eight miles south of Hollister, sits on the main San Andreas fault. Here, walls, floor slabs and concrete drainage ditches are being offset in one of the most remarkable examples of slow creep along the entire San Andreas fault. Opposite sides of the fault move past each other at an average rate of about one-half inch per year. (For information on the winery's hours of operation and tours, call 408-636-9143.)

The San Andreas and the Calaveras faults join together just south of Paicines. The combined zone is three or four miles wide, with ample evidence of complex fault movements and rock displacement. Dislocated mountain slivers show up in the flat fault valley along State Highway 25. The first is along Cienega Road about a mile and half north of the Old Airline Road intersection; and the second is just west of the Old Airline Road-State Highway 25 intersection.

In Little Rabbit Valley, a good exposure of dull-reddish volcanic rock shows up in a State Highway 25 road cut. This is basement (oldest) rock east of the fault that has been forced to the surface at this one point by repeated fault movements. As State Highway 25 approaches the Coalinga Road intersection, it is paralleled by a broken escarpment and several sag areas on the east side of the roadway. On Coalinga Road itself, a conspicuous escarpment overlooks a narrow, closed depression a few hundred yards east of the intersection with State Highway 25. These features mark the line of

The 1966 Parkfield earthquake offset the center line on Highway 46 by two inches (left); additional creep during the next two months lengthened the offset to five inches (right). Photos courtesy University of California EERC Library.

most recent activity within the wide fault zone.

5. PARKFIELD. This tiny community of 34 population is the center of a major government study that could impact earthquake prediction in the entire state. Since 1857, six moderate-size quakes of magnitude 6.0 have happened here on the average of once every 22 years—an unusually regular pattern. The last three in 1934, 1944, and 1966 were almost identical. On the assumption that another M6.0 quake was due again in the 1987-1993 time period, a complex network of instrumentation has been installed since 1985 in an attempt to catch the quake in the act. If the plan works, and a large quake falls into the net, the information collected before, during and after the fault movement will be the best data set available in the world.

Evidence of horizontal movement in this area is visible at the Parkfield Bridge that straddles the San Andreas fault. The west end of the bridge has moved northwest more than 30 inches since construction in 1932; the concrete surface of the bridge and steel guard rails are bent accordingly.

Cholame Valley is a sunken block between two active branches of the San Andreas fault zone. The western branch is visible as a low, discontinuous scarp at the base of the ridge bordering the valley. South of Cholame, a row of impressive scarps and offset stream channels is visible west of Davis Road (the best example is 1. 1 miles south of State Highway 46). From here,

the fault follows Palo Prieto Pass, marked by several more offset stream channels and sag areas.

6. CARRIZO PLAIN. This undrained north-south depression is six miles wide and 50 miles long, between State Highways 58 and 166. It is one of the best areas in the world to see fault features. Along the eastern edge of the plain is a spectacular collection of old scarps that are the result of hundreds of fault movements, smaller scarplets caused by the 1857 earthquake, large sag ponds, and a long series of offset drainage channels. Some streams were offset up to 22 feet in 1857 alone.

This desolate country has mostly unpaved roads and no services of any kind, so it is suitable only for the most determined fault explorers. Most of the are is preserved in the Carrizo Plain Natural Area. The Goodwin Visitor Center on Soda Lake Road, 15 miles south of State Highway 58, is a good place to start a tour. It has excellent displays on the geography, wildlife and geology of the region, and can provide a map with the location of the San Andreas fault, the plain's elusive road network, and directions to an overlook at Wallace Creek, one of the most dramatically offset streams anywhere along the fault. (The Natural Area is open year round. The Visitor Center is open only from October through May; for details on days and hours, plus local road conditions, phone 805-475-2131).

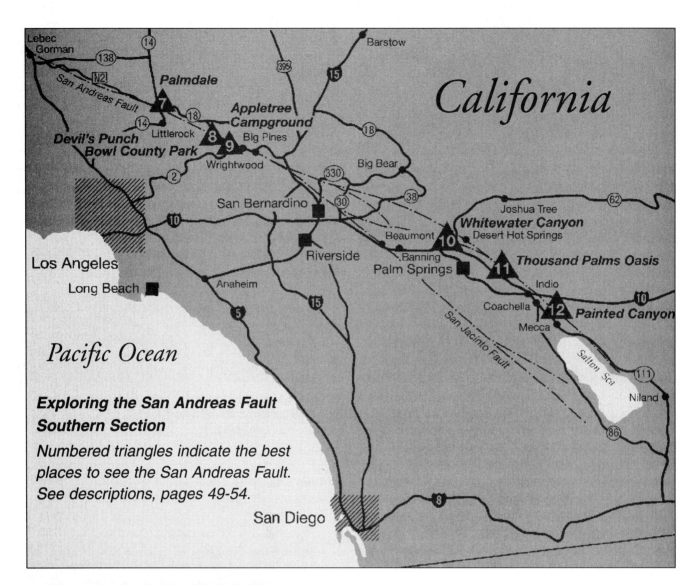

Exploring the San Andreas Fault Southern Section

Numbered triangles indicate the best places to see the San Andreas Fault. See descriptions, pages 49–54.

Interstate 5 cuts through the San Andreas Fault at Tejon Pass. The line of most recent activity shows up as a band of black "gouge" in the road cut (arrow). In the background, the fault follows the line of telephone poles into Gorman.

Elkhorn Scarp, a steep cliff formed by repeated fault movements, looms up at the eastern edge of Carrizo Plain. In the background is the Temblor Range.

The Southern Section

South of State Highway 166, the fault is traceable through Santiago Creek Canyon, San Emidgio Canyon and Cuddy Valley into Frazier Park. Within Cuddy Valley, several scarps and sag ponds are visible from the road.

Near Frazier Park, the San Andreas fault zone intersects with the Garlock fault, which is significant both for its length and its lack of activity. The Garlock is a left-lateral strike-slip fault that extends eastward at least 175 miles from Frazier Park. Slip rate for the central segment of the Garlock is close to 1-1/2 inches a year, giving it the potential of producing large quakes about every 500 to 1,000 years. However, it has been quiet for the last two centuries. The largest quake recorded on this fault zone was in 1992 with a magnitude of 5.7. It occurred 11 days after the Landers quake (see page 115) and may have been triggered by it.

Tejon Pass is the northernmost of three freeway passes revealing the San Andreas fault. Interstate 5 cuts a deep slice right out of the heart of the fault zone, characterized by a band of black gouge (crushed and discolored rocks) in the road cut east of the freeway that defines the line of most recent activity. These features are best seen from the summit of the old highway (Peace Valley Road), accessible from the Gorman or Frazier Park turnoffs.

Just south of Tejon Pass, the fault passes through a saddle marked by a line of telephone poles, and then parallels Gorman Post Road, where it is visible as a line of sag ponds. Between Gorman and Palmdale, the fault parallels State Highway 138 as far as Quail Lake, then continues on a straight line through Pine and Oakdale Canyons, the Lake Hughes area and Leona Canyon. County Road N2 follows the valley. There are few readily visible fault features other than exposures of crystalline rocks, crushed and chemically altered until they are little more than white powder held together in loose clumps. Just west of the town of Leona Valley, recent fault activity formed a side-hill ridge in the mountain slope, and a number of offset stream beds are visible north of the road.

7. PALMDALE. State Highway 14 (the Antelope Valley freeway) is the second major highway to cut through the San Andreas fault zone, this time just south of Palmdale. The Lamont Odett Overlook on the east side of the freeway about two miles north of the Pearblossom Highway exit is at the edge of the fault zone. Visitors look down onto Palmdale Reservoir, a large sag pond dammed in the 1890s to increase its water-storage capacity. Two plaques help interpret the topography.

North of the Overlook a dramatic roadcut reveals

THE SAN JACINTO FAULT

The San Jacinto fault zone makes up the southern branch of the San Andreas system. Well-defined, it has been very active in recent geologic times.

After diverging from the main San Andreas fault near Palmdale, the San Jacinto fault passes through Devil's Punchbowl (see description below) and then is visible again at two sites along the Angeles Crest Highway (State Highway 2). The first, a few miles south of County Road N4, is Inspiration Point, where a plaque explains how the San Gabriel river splits into the Prairie Fork and Vincent Gulch branches along the eroded fault zone. The second exposure another three miles to the south is Vincent Gap, where highway cuts through the fault reveal a brilliantly colored line of red sedimentary rocks butted against gray granitics.

The fault then passes through San Bernardino, under both the campus of San Bernardino Valley College and the elevated intersection of Interstates 10 and 215, and down the west side of the Salton Basin. Movements along this fault have formed a huge underground dam (known locally as Bunker Hill) that trapped great quantities of water tapped by San Bernardino's founders. The Saint Elias Greek Orthodox Church sits on the highest part of a double-sided scarp that arises abruptly from the flat terrain just north of the Colton Avenue-Coburn Avenue intersection.

Farther south, one strand of the fault zone runs along the base of the steep and straight slopes of the San Jacinto Mountains. Both Gilman and Soboba Hot Springs use water dammed along the fault; vertical displacement here is more than 1,000 feet. Another strand lies between San Jacinto and Hemet.

The San Jacinto Fault has been the most active branch of the southern San Andreas system; it has produced at least nine earthquakes of M6 0 or greater in historic times. Among the largest were Fish Creek Mountains (M6 6) in 1942, Borrego Mountain (M6.5) in 1968, and Superstition Hills (M6.6) in 1987.

In White Wash, southeast of Anza, the San Jacinto Fault is marked by a clear contrast of rock types. Older rocks above the fault apparently moved upward in relation to more recent gravels. Clarence R. Allen photo.

the fault's twisting and folding action (see photo on page 53). For the most dramatic view, take the Avenue S off-ramp from the freeway, park on the west side and walk north on dirt paths to the top of the ridge that was sliced in two by the highway. Rocks exposed in the cut are spectacularly folded and faulted, with a wide band of gouge at the south end. The 1857 quake caused a 20-foot-long rupture here and created a low escarpment just south of the main ridge. Between Palmdale and Cajon Pass, the fault cuts a straight line through the northern slopes of the San Gabriel Mountains, marked by an almost continuous chain of scarps and sag ponds. East of Palmdale, near Pearblossom, is Pallett Creek, a small, dramatically offset stream with a 20-foot-deep channel that provided the exposures needed to establish dates of earthquakes on the San Andreas fault during the past 2,000 years (see page 124).

Little Rock Creek between Palmdale and Littlerock has been significantly offset by repeated fault action over the last 50,000 years—so great in fact that is impossible to visualize from ground level without walking its curved route. West of the Angeles Natonal Forest Ranger Station at Valyermo, a line of trees and springs can be seen along an escarpment that probably dates from 1857.

8. THE DEVIL'S PUNCHBOWL. This county park preserves a spectacular exposure of weathered conglomerate rocks on the south side of the San Andreas fault that are very similar to the Cajon Beds north of the fault in

In Pacoima Canyon, the San Gabriel Fault forms a clean dividing line between two contrasting rock types; at right is gneiss, at left is granodiroite. This unlikely face-to-face contact has been created by long-term fault movements. Photo by C. W. Jennings.

Lone Pine Canyon. The once-horizontal rock formations have been tilted, broken and uplifted by fault action, and then eroded by wind and water. The Devil's Punchbowl formations also abut the San Jacinto fault (opposite page); it is clearly exposed at the base of the cliff where the Devil's Chair is located.

9. APPLETREE CAMPGROUND. Just southeast of Appletree Campground, on Big Pine Highway in Angeles National Forest, a creek has cut a deep notch through the fault, exposing granite crushed to powder by fault movement. To reach the site, park at the campground and walk up the road at the east end of the parking area to the water tower where you can look down into a broad area of pulverized rock, or even take a short walk down inside the fault zone.

The San Andreas fault reaches its highest elevation in California at Big Pines Summit, at the intersection of County Road N4 and State Highway 2. A concrete tower just west of the Angeles National Forest Ranger Station marks the spot at above 6,800 feet. At Big Pines saddle, an escarpment probably caused by the 1857 earthquake lies north of the intersection and extends beyond the Ranger Station to the east.

Back on County Road N4, just east of Mountain High ski area, is a large patch of willows and other swampy plants on the south side of the road. They

A LOOK AT OTHER SOUTHERN CALIFORNIA FAULTS

Southern Californians have these opportunities to see "inside" some of the area's lesser faults.

Sierra Madre Fault Zone

At the base of the San Gabriel Mountains is the Sierra Madre fault zone. One of the branches of these east-west trending faults is visible in the Arcadia Wilderness Park in Arcadia. Take the Santa Anita Avenue offramp from Interstate 210 (the Foothill Freeway), drive north for about 1.3 miles, turn right on Elkins Avenue and then left on Highland Oaks Drive. The entrance to the Wilderness Park is about a mile north. Park alongside the creek and look at the escarpment across the way. The fault line is visible as a vertical line between two disparate rock types; some minor sliding covers a section of the break. (The Wilderness Park is open from 8 a. m. to Sunset, Monday-Friday only.)

San Fernando Fault

Movement on the San Fernando fault was responsible for the devastating 1971 earthquake. One place to see its effect on the landscape is on Blucher Avenue, the frontage road on the west side of U. S. 405 (the San Diego Freeway) just north of the Rinaldi Avenue exit. Two branches of the fault are visible in the road cut, and shale crushed by fault action has spilled out on the road as shattered, soft rocks.

San Gabriel Fault

The San Gabriel fault is clearly visible in Pacoima Canyon along Little Tujunga Road in Angeles National Forest, where the fault slices between two massive rock formations. To reach the site, take the Osborne Street exit from State Highway 210, and follow Little Tujunga Road about 10 miles to a Forest Service marker. A short trail leads to the fault site, visible just left of the waterfall.

Tuna Canyon Fault

This fault zone crosses Topanga Canyon north of Pacific Coast Highway. From Pacific Coast Highway, take Topanga Canyon Boulevard for 2.2 miles, park just north of the bridge at the entrance to the narrows, and walk north along the road. There are several branches within the half-mile-wide zone, but the southernmost branch clearly separates easily recognizable reddish-brown conglomerate rock beds from sloping light-colored layers of sandstone. A thin band of gouge and intruded basaltic igneous rock appears between the rocks. One especially noticeable intrusion is right along the eastern edge of creek bed.

One of the most spectacular examples of folded and faulted rock beds on the north side of the San Andreas fault is exposed in the State Route 14 road cut just south of Palmdale, on the southern margin of the Mojave Desert. Robert E. Wallace photo.

thrive on water trapped in an area of crushed rock within the San Andreas fault that has dammed water and forced it to the surface. Southeast of Wrightwood, the fault can be traced through Lone Pine Canyon, where linear features and series of low escarpments are clearly related to erosion along the fault. The southern end of the surface break caused by the 1857 quake was somewhere east of Wrightwood.

At Cajon Pass, Interstate 15 is the third major freeway to cut through the San Andreas fault zone, revealing a large area of crushed and distorted rock, similar to those seen in the roadcuts of Interstate 5 at Tejon Pass and State Highway 14 near Palmdale. Pink outcrops of the Cajon Beds, so similar to the formations in Devils Punchbowl County Park, are visible on both sides of the freeway near the intersection with State Highway 138.

South and east of Cajon Pass, the San Andreas fault system becomes much broader and more complex. The northern section of the system, labeled the San Andreas, lies northeast of Interstate 15 and then Interstate 215. The line of most recent activity is recognizable as a conspicuous offset in Cable Canyon and in other nearby ravines, and by an escarpment and line of brush and trees in Devil Canyon.

The Glen Helen fault is sub-parallel to the San Andreas System; it lies at the base of Lower Lytle Creek Ridge and forms the southern edge of Cajon Wash; a prominent scarp crosses Devore Road in Glen Helen Regional Park.

At Waterman Canyon (very near State Highway 18), the main San Andreas fault zone splits into two identifiable branches, the San Andreas and Mill Creek faults. San Bernardino National Forest's Del Rosa Ranger Station is located on a low ridge squeezed up between these two branches that at this point are very close together.

East of San Bernardino, the San Andreas branch passes just north of Highland Avenue and again is visible where Greenspot Road crosses the Santa Ana wash. On the east side of the canyon the brownish gravels exposed in the cliff are contrasted against gray granitic rocks slanted north about 50 degrees. A grove of sycamore trees identifies an area where ground water is dammed by the fault.

State Highway 38 crosses the San Andreas branch between San Bernardino National Forest's Mill Creek Ranger Station and the mouth of Mill Creek Canyon. Obvious differences in rock types and colors indicate opposite sides of the fault, with white granitic rocks on the north; tilted, reddish sandstones on the south. East of Mountain Home Village campground the road turns

The San Andreas Fault cuts a spectacularly straight gash through the Indio Hills, made of rock beds tilted and thrust upward by long-term earth movements. *Spence Air Photos.*

to follow the straight line of the Mill Creek fault all the way to Forest Falls. The San Andreas branch passes through the Oak Glen area and loses definition at Burro Flat north of Banning.

Along the south fork of the White Water River the Mill Creek fault appears to phase into the Mission Creek fault, which in turn heads through Desert Hot Springs. Three large scarps east of town are visible from the intersection of Dillon and Mountain View Roads.

Another branch of this complex area, the Banning fault, first becomes identifiable in the slopes above Beaumont. It appears as the major structural break on the north side of San Gorgonio Pass, a deep gash between the rugged slopes of the San Gorgonio and San Jacinto mountains, the two highest peaks in Southern California. The pass owes its existence to complex fault activity. It appears to be narrow block that has not been elevated as far as the steep escarpments on either side.

10. WHITEWATER CANYON. The Banning fault makes a conspicuous appearance in Whitewater Canyon, where a distinct band of vegetation marks its route across the canyon floor. The main road passes close to the western slopes, so the marked differences of the gray granitic

rocks north of the fault and the brownish gravels to the south is very apparent. At the end of Whitewater Canyon is a spectacular exposure of conglomerate beds tilted by fault action and then pitted and shaped by wind and water.

The Banning branch shows up again as a swath of brush and trees, and a parallel series of scarplets and troughs near the intersection of Palm Drive and 20th Avenue in the otherwise-arid Seven Palms Valley.

11. THOUSAND PALMS OASIS. The Coachella Valley Preserve that covers 13,000 acres of the Indio Hills has its headquarters at Thousand Palms oasis, on Thousand Palms Road on the northern side of the Indio Hills. This is a good source of information on the area and can also provide a welcome respite from desert heat. The oasis is fed by water seeping up along the Mission Creek fault (for hours of operation and tours, call 619-343-2733).

The Indio Hills themselves are fault-controlled. Only 20 miles long and two or three miles wide, they have been squeezed and tilted out of the flat desert by the shearing action of fault movements. Squeezing tilted the beds; erosion has rounded and pitted the layers. Chemical oxidation, wind, and sun provided the range of colors.

San Andreas fault cuts a sharp line through the Mecca Hills in the Coachella Valley. Both the 1968 Borrego Mountain and 1979 Imperial Valley earthquakes created related movement along this section of the fault zone. Photo by Robert E. Wallace.

Trees in Biskra Palms hug the lowest elevations where roots can reach down into water impounded along the fault.

Thousand Palms Road also crosses the Banning fault on the southeastern side of the Indio Hills; Willis Palms marks the site of a spring caused by movement along the fault.

Northeast of the town of Indio, the Banning and Mission Creek branches converge into a single zone, again called the San Andreas, along the southern edge of the Indio Hills. Damming ground water on the uphill (north) side has given rise to a very straight line of palm trees and small oases, the largest of which is Biskra Palms.

12. PAINTED CANYON. The San Andreas is pretty much a single line again as it crosses this beautiful exposure of uplifted and tilted sedimentary rocks on the southwestern edge of the Mecca Hills, northeast of the town of Mecca. The unpaved, graded road into the canyon passes through towering cliffs folded and thrust into weird shapes, then weathered into a colorful array of shadowy caves and bright highlights. The most recent trace of the fault is evidenced by the reddish hill on the right at the entrance to the canyon. The Mecca Hills are made up of similar formations of normally flat sedimentary beds squeezed up by movements within the fault zone.

State Highway 111 parallels the fault on the eastern edge of the Salton Sea. At Salt Creek bridge, shales and pink sandstones are clearly separated and a wide band of reddish gouge is visible. Near Bombay Beach, the southernmost trace of the San Andreas fault dies out with a whimper in the desert sands.

A reddish hill at the entrance to Painted Canyon marks the line of most recent activity within the San Andreas fault zone. Rock beds in the background have been tilted by fault movements.

A man stands on steeply inclined zone of reddish gouge marking Hidden Springs fault zone, a branch of the San Andreas fault system in the Mecca Hills. Rocks at right are nearly horizontal conglomerates and sandstones; rocks left of the fault are crushed volcanics and granitics. Photo by John C. Crowell.

The path of the San Andreas fault through southern California's arid deserts is marked by a long series of oases that have developed where ground water has been impounded behind the underground barrier created by repeated fault movements.

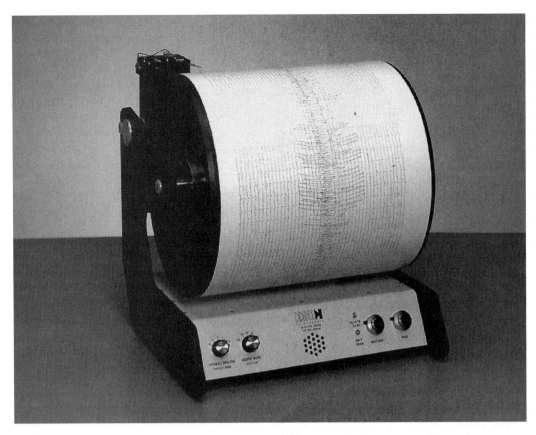

Direct-write drum recorders provide a graphic picture of earthquake waves; a pen or stylus writes fine, reliable traces of major and minor movements. Digital recording devices are gradually replacing these units, to increase accuracy and better enable the computers to record and analyze the broad spectrum of earthquake waves. Photo courtesy Kinemetrics Inc.

After a major quake, portable seismic recorders are installed in the epicentral area to record aftershock patterns and the velocity of these shocks. The seismograph is enclosed in a cylinder (arrow) that usually is buried in the ground so it can pick up the faintest movements. Photo courtesy Kinemetrics Inc.

Earthquake Mechanics & Measurements

Chapter 3

Despite attention paid to San Francisco and Oakland in the 1989 Loma Prieta quake, Watsonville and other towns in the epicentral area around Monterey Bay received most of the shaking. Design and construction defects were quickly revealed as the shaking brought down buildings that did not incorporate modern seismic safeguards. Photo by Mark Gibson.

Despite California's hundreds of detectable earthquakes every year, the exact nature of faults and earthquakes is not completely understood. It is difficult to arrive at a consensus among geologists and seismologists about fault-plane characteristics, reasons faults rupture in the first place, why ruptures start and stop where they do, and characteristics of the movement. New theories currently being debated may result in some significant changes in scientific thought.

The most widely accepted model of earthquake generation is *elastic rebound*—the slow build-up and sudden release of strain within masses of rock. As the Pacific and North American plates drift slowly past each other (see page 22), strain is introduced into the rocks on both sides of the fault zone. Opposing the steady strain build-up is the basic elastic strength of the rocks. Even though they may become deformed and their positions distorted by the stress, rocks tend to hold their basic positions and the fault remains "glued" together by friction. The deformation is encompassed within a zone about 30 miles wide on each side of the fault. It is greatest right along the fault and decreases to about half the maximum at a distance of 20 miles.

Eventually, strain build-up becomes so great that it overcomes the strength of the rocks. Then the earth moves along the interface—the fault plane—and masses of rock on opposite sides of the fault suddenly and quickly scrape past each other to relieve the stress and allow the rock formations to regain equilibrium.

Fault movement can be compared to snapping your fingers. Push the fingers together, and the friction keeps them from moving. Push harder, overcome this friction, and the fingers move suddenly, releasing energy in the form of sound waves that travel from your fingers to your ears. Similarly, when stress builds up in the rocks on opposite sides of the fault, the rocks are pushed sideways, but do not slip gradually. It is only when enough pressure is built up and the rocks move that the energy is released as seismic waves that cause the shaking we feel as an earthquake.

The amount of "snapping back" along the fault varies. Most of the time, resistance of rocks along a fault is weak, the earth moves after a slight build-up of elastic strain, and the resulting earthquake is small. If the rocks are strong or locked tightly together, pressures may build for a hundred years or longer. When stress finally becomes great enough to overcome the tight bond—and it most certainly will—pressure is released like the uncoiling of a giant spring. The jarring movement of the rocks sliding past each other creates a major quake. The San Andreas fault is weak and tends to break under relatively low stress, yet it creates some great earthquakes. This may be due to easy slippage along smooth rock faces that tend to perpetuate the quake.

Another theory postulates that small earthquakes generally occur on short faults or fault segments where the resistance of the rocks is strong—not weak—and any movement is brief and restricted to a small area because

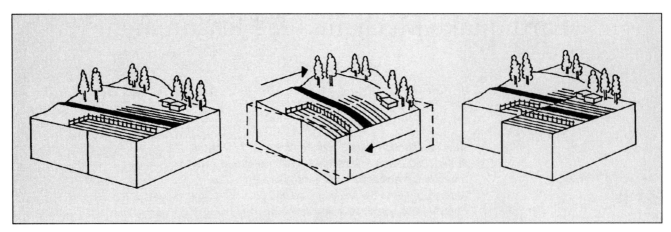

According to the elastic-rebound theory, a fault is incapable of movement until strain has built up in the rocks on either side. This strain is accumulated by the gradual shifting of the earth's tectonic plates (at a rate of about two inches a year along the San Andreas Fault). Rocks become distorted but hold their original positions until accumulated stress finally overcomes the resistance of the rocks and the earth snaps back into an unstrained position. Sudden movement of the rocks past each other causes the shock waves we know as earthquakes. A major earth movement is never a single event. There are sometimes foreshocks, and always aftershocks, as an entire region adjusts itself.

the pressure tends to limit the rupture. Larger earthquakes are more likely to occur on longer, well-developed faults where the rock faces may be smoother. Once movement starts, it tends to continue a greater distance before encountering enough resistance to stop.

The amount of energy released is related to the total surface area of the fault plane that slips, the amount of the displacement, and the rigidity of the rocks. The largest quakes are generated in subduction zones (see page 22). It is generally agreed that the 1857 and 1906 quakes represent the largest we can expect on the San Andreas fault.

A recent study of 50 large quakes indicated that all began slowly and then released most of their energy in a burst. It's not known exactly what determines why, when, and where fault movement stops.

Fault Movements

The point where a fault rupture starts is called the *hypocenter* or *focus*; the spot on the surface directly above the hypocenter is called the *epicenter*. Earthquakes are described as *shallow*, with a hypocenter less than 50 miles deep; *intermediate*, originating at about 50 to 180 miles; and *deep*, below 180 miles. All movements deeper than 50 miles originate in subduction zones, where great slabs of shallow lithosphere are sinking into the Earth's mantle as

part of plate-tectonic motion.

All California quakes are shallow-focus events, except for the few associated with the Cascadia Subduction Zone near Cape Mendocino. Northern California has the shallowest with an average of about six miles (there are exceptions—the 1989 Loma Prieta quake originated 10 miles deep). Southern California quakes tend to be deeper, down to 12 miles.

An earthquake is not generated by movement at a single point; fault rupture starts at one place, the hypocenter. Then it propagates along the fault plane—sometimes in one direction, sometimes both—at speeds up to two miles per second, or 7,200 miles per hour. The break continues along the fault plane until its energy is overcome by some resistance or a cross structure, and it stops.

The area of the fault plane that is broken is called the *rupture surface*. The total length that breaks has a key effect on both magnitude and intensities. In an M5 quake, the actual rupturing process is over in a few seconds, even though we might continue to feel movement for a longer period as the seismic waves bounce back and forth off subsurface geologic structures. In an M8.0 quake, as much as 250 miles of the fault can break. At the rate of two miles per second, it will take more than two minutes for the rupture to propagate from one end of the fracture

Rows of trees in orange grove near Mexican border were straight until May 18, 1940, when the Imperial Valley earthquake suddenly disrupted the pattern with one giant lurch to create a graphic example of elastic rebound. Horizontal displacement was 10 feet within the grove (removed several years ago), and as much as 19 feet in farm lands farther south.

zone to the other.

Fault movements can be horizontal, vertical or a combination of the two. The San Andreas fault apparently has gone through long periods of both vertical and horizontal movement. Most recent events have been predominantly horizontal. The 1857 and 1906 earthquakes produced horizontal movements that reached 20 feet or more at the surface. Vertical displacements were rare, and seldom exceeded three or four feet.

Measurements of fault movements are always stated in relative terms. When movement is vertical, there can be either an uplift on the earth on one side of the fault, or a depression of the earth on the opposite side. In some cases, both actions may occur simultaneously. Horizontal measurements need the same careful description. Along the San Andreas fault, the coastal (western) portion of California is said to move north in relation to the continental side that lies to the east, though there is no way of determining which side actually moves. Modern measuring techniques using Global Positioning Satellites (see page 130) are expected to reveal exactly which plates do the moving in a future quake.

Foreshocks

Fault movements resulting in major earthquakes are never isolated events. In addition to the main break, there are smaller movements on the same or related faults as an entire area of subsurface rock makes minor adjustments relating to the biggest movement.

In any series of quakes, the one with the largest magnitude is called the *main shock*. Smaller quakes in the days or weeks preceding it are called *foreshocks* and smaller quakes afterward are called *aftershocks*. In some cases, if a subsequent quake with a larger magnitude comes along in the same area and appears to be generated by the same fault, what was thought to be main shock can turn into a foreshock. This happened in 1992 when the April 23 Joshua Tree earthquake turned out to be a foreshock of the Landers earthquake of June 28.

Foreshock patterns could be valuable data in earthquake prediction, if only they were consistent and predictable. Unfortunately, they are difficult to categorize. Only after a major earthquake has run its course can seismologists go back over the seismic records and identify foreshocks. And the analysis can be more confusing than revealing. Foreshocks can occur months, weeks or a few hours in advance of a major earthquake—but most often not at all. Recent research indicates that there may be some preliminary movement just seconds before a major

As the 1906 earthquake propagated northward from the epicenter near San Francisco, the surface rupture passed within a mile of Fort Ross. This old wood church was flattened by the strong waves. Photo by Mary Hill, California Division of Mines and Geology.

fault break, but usually it is very slight and difficult to detect.

None of the earthquakes originating on the reverse faults in the Transverse Ranges (see page 28) have produced recognizable foreshocks. However, 44% of the strike-slip quakes originating there, and 35% of the moderate and large earthquakes on the strike-slip San Andreas fault were preceded by some foreshock activity.

Hopefully, data gathered from future quakes, especially the next one at Parkfield (see page 47), will shed more light on this critical, highly elusive aspect of California's seismicity.

Aftershocks

Aftershocks are much more common than foreshocks. Their number, size and frequency are among the most predictable elements of the earthquake sequence. Every major shock is followed by a series of aftershocks of varying strengths, with frequency and magnitude related to the main event.

They can occur close to the original hypocenter, on other segments of the same fault, and on other faults in nearby areas as a large region readjusts itself. Aftershock patterns provide a general idea of the size of the fault that ruptured in the earthquake with a three-dimensional "picture" that even helps define the dip of the fault plane.

In general, bigger earthquakes have more and larger aftershocks. Age of the fault also seems to play a role. Earthquakes on the San Andreas, an old and well-developed fault, have fewer aftershocks than quakes on younger thrust faults.

A large fault movement relieves the pressure along a fault or some part of it, and also changes the stress patterns for miles around, leading to a chain reaction. Aftershocks may continue for weeks, months or years with the greatest number and largest size concentrated close enough to the main shake to cause panic among people who fear a repeat of the main event.

A typical California earthquake of M5.8 can be expected to produce 26 aftershocks of about M3.0 during the first 24 hours and 41 in the first 10 days. Even as the magnitudes tend to decrease, the aftershock zones tend to widen with time, as the post-earthquake adjustment spreads over a larger area. Both the 1971 San Fernando and 1994 Northridge earthquakes generated more than 5,000 measurable aftershocks within the first 30 days. Rarely, an aftershock may be almost as large as the main quake; an August 22, 1952, aftershock of the July 21 Kern County quake caused more damage in Bakersfield than the original, main tremor (see page 100).

The precision of aftershock prediction has been helpful in emergency response efforts in recent earthquakes.

Much damage in the 1940 Imperial Valley quake was caused by aftershocks that knocked down older buildings significantly weakened by the main event. Photo courtesy University of California EERC Library.

Firemen, policemen, utility-repair crews and others involved in damage control are kept alert of the probability of aftershocks and their size—valuable information when implementing emergency programs and anticipating further problems.

How do we know whether an earthquake is an aftershock of a previous quake, or a brand-new event? Proximity of the epicenter and recency of the second quake compared to the first are the main criteria, along with the actual aftershock pattern compared to statistical models of previous quakes of the same size. Three quakes in the Los Angeles area on December 6, 1994 were determined to be aftershocks of the January 17 Northridge quakes; one was M4.5 and was the 57th aftershock of M4.0 or greater resulting from the original January event.

Sometimes, what appears to be an aftershock turns out to be a "triggered" earthquake of an entirely different motion on a different fault. This happened in the Superstition Hills Sequence of 1987, at Cape Mendocino in 1992, and at Landers in 1992.

Earthquake Measurements

Earthquakes are measured in two ways: Magnitude, an expression of energy at the source, and intensity, the actual effects at specific locations. The first is based on instrument records, the second on personal observations. Although they are separate measurements, they are often confused by the news media and the public.

Magnitude

Magnitude is an expression of the amount of energy released at an earthquake's source, and is expressed as an ordinal number (M3.1, M7.6, etc.). Numbers are based on records made on seismographs that record seismic waves in three directions: north-south, east-west, up-down. This combination tells the seismologist the general direction of the seismic-wave source, size of the fault break at its source, and character of the wave motion.

Modern digital-recording seismographic systems, constant computer monitoring of hundreds of seismographic stations in California, and sophisticated analysis of the speed of seismic waves in different kinds of rock, make it possible to determine the epicenter of the earthquake and assign a preliminary magnitude very shortly after the shaking starts. The only limiting factor is how long the

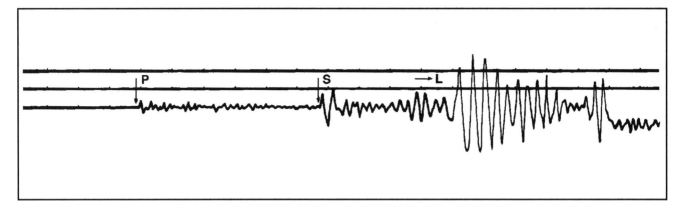

The seismogram above was recorded at the University of California Seismographic Station in Berkeley. Source of these seismic waves was 2,550 miles away—a quake of magnitude 6.5 in the Aleutian Islands. It clearly shows the three types of waves generated by a major quake.

READING A SEISMOGRAM

Energy released by fault movements takes the form of seismic waves that radiate out in all directions. These are similar to waves created when you drop a pebble into a pond or tap the side of a bowl of gelatin. However, these simple demonstrations are vast understatements. Earthquake waves are generated by large masses of rock moving past each other. They travel through the earth, somewhat like ocean waves, and when they reach the surface, they truly fit the description of "an irresistible force."

Seismic waves that cause earthquakes are complex. There are three types, each with a unique character and mode of travel:

P waves are primary sound waves. Fastest of the three, they are the first to reach the surface. P waves radiate out from the hypocenter at about 3.5 miles per second in the earth's crust, and about 8 miles per second through its molten core. They compress and dilate rock, with a "push-pull" effect that causes the earth to move back and forth quickly in the same direction that the waves are traveling.

S waves are secondary, slower shear waves—about 2 miles per second— that cause the earth to move at right angles to the direction the waves are traveling, so the ground and structures may move sideways. S waves cannot pass through liquids, so they do not penetrate the molten core of the earth, and do not travel through large lakes or oceans.

L waves are slow, long-period surface waves that resemble ripples of water on the surface of a pond and are distinguishable only outside the immediate shock area. There are two types: *Love waves* that move the ground (but not liquids) from side to side, with potentially significant damage to structural foundations; and *Rayleigh waves* that seem to "roll" forward through rock and water, causing both vertical and horizontal movement that can damage the superstructures of tall buildings, even those at some distance from the epicenter.

P and S waves travel through the earth, and L waves travel around the earth's surface. Speeds of both P and S waves are affected by different types of rocks and soils, and are significantly faster in solid rock than soft soils. Passing from rock to soil, the waves slow down and increase in amplitude.

Structures and people on soft soil will experience more intense shaking for a longer time than those on hard rock at the same distance from the fault movement. The looser and deeper the soil, the greater the amplification.

These waves lose much of their energy as they travel over great distances, but sensitive detectors (seismometers) record waves emitted by even the smallest of quakes and magnify them electronically. There are both strong-motion seismometers, activated only by significant signals, and continuously recording sensitive devices that can detect small movements even at great distances.

The seismometers are connected to a system that produces a permanent recording, called a seismograph. The first arrival of each type of wave is easy to distinguish on a seismograph, and their differences in speed and character reveal the nature of the earthquake. P waves arrive first; when the S waves start, their amplitude is 2-3 times larger than the P waves; finally the long, slow surface waves show up. This leads to the characteristic shape of a seismogram, shown here. Because P waves travel faster, the time between the arrival of the P and S waves increases

FAMOUS MAGNITUDES

Here are the magnitudes of California's most famous earthquakes, adjusted to the moment magnitude scale in almost all cases:

7.8	January 9, 1857, Tejon Pass
7.7	April 18, 1906, San Francisco
7.6	March 26, 1872, Owens Valley
7.5	July 21, 1952, Kern County
7.3	June 28, 1992, Landers
7.1	April 25, 1992, Cape Mendocino
6.9	October 17, 1989, Loma Prieta
6.7	February 9, 1971, San Fernando
6.7	January 17, 1994, Northridge
6.5	May 2, 1983, Coalinga
6.3	June 29, 1925, Santa Barbara
6.2	March 10, 1933, Long Beach
6.2	June 28, 1992, Big Bear

If these magnitudes recorded over the last 200 years also are typical of earthquakes for the last 2,000 years, it is assumed that we will never have an M8.0 earthquake in California. It is conceivable that the San Andreas Fault could break from Parkfield down to the Coachella Valley. That could well result in a magnitude of 8.0+, but it is highly unlikely.

as distance increases from the source. This is directly comparable to the time lag between seeing lightning and hearing thunder.

Wave size on the seismograph, and the time interval between the arrival of the first P and the first S wave indicates the magnitude of the quake and the distance between the epicenter and the seismogram. A seismographic record becomes jumbled after a few minutes as the waves intermingle; the first arrival times are critical.

The method of locating the source of an earthquake is to determine the time interval between the P and S wave arrivals at several seismographic stations; computers linked to the recording stations analyze the data and locate the epicenter in a few minutes or less.

Depending on their location and their ability to recognize an earthquake the instant it starts, even laymen can sometimes recognize the difference in the shock waves. It is common to hear reports of "two separate shocks, a few seconds apart" or apparently conflicting stories of "a short up-and-down motion" in one area and "a long rolling motion" in another. These are nothing more than responses to the different seismic waves caused by the same event.

Those closest to the epicenter will tend to feel the brief, strong shock of the P waves, followed closely by the stronger S waves. At 20 miles from the epicenter, the P and S waves may arrive 4 seconds apart, and at a distance of 50 miles the lapse will be an even more significant 10 seconds. Those farther from the epicenter will experience a different sensation; in general, the period of shaking will be longer, with more of a rolling motion.

Most often, though, the waves are jumbled and complex when they shake the surface. When the P and S waves "bounce" off different rock types and other discontinuities within the earth, they change their character and speeds and become intermingled with each other and with the surface waves.

Also, the waves do not stop after the first break; the quake will continue to generate energy as the rupture moves along the fault. Also, the fault movement may not have been a single event; there may be two or more breaks in quick succession, each with its own wave patterns. So the motion felt some distance from the epicenter may consist of two or more sets of primary waves, plus refracted shocks that reinforce or cancel each other in a jumble of rock-

ing, rolling and sideways movements.

It has often been stated that earthquakes are not capricious, and there are good reasons why one structure stands and another falls. However, an increasing amount of evidence, especially from the 1989 and 1994 earthquakes, indicates that energy focus at specific locations is influenced by underground geology.

As the complex P and S waves travel through the earth at different speeds and are reflected and refracted by differences in rock, soil and water barriers, they come together haphazardly at certain points with much greater strength than normal for the given soil conditions. This can cause some well-constructed buildings, even those on solid rock, to break up unexpectedly.

Conversely, there are "troughs" where the energy is diminished, and normally susceptible structures escape undamaged. These variations are impossible to forecast, and indicate that earthquake damage can include a capricious element after all.

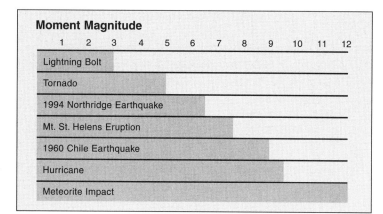

Moment Magnitude

	1	2	3	4	5	6	7	8	9	10	11	12
Lightning Bolt												
Tornado												
1994 Northridge Earthquake												
Mt. St. Helens Eruption												
1960 Chile Earthquake												
Hurricane												
Meteorite Impact												

MOMENT MAGNITUDES

In addition to providing accurate measurements of current earthquakes, the moment magnitude scale allows seismologists to make two other important computations:

1. Seismic moment can be computed either from instrumental records or from geologic field measurements along the fault. By using both instrument and field records, magnitudes of earthquakes that occurred early in California's recorded history can be estimated.

This valuable scientific data has caused adjustment in some of our favorite numbers. To students of history, the 1906 San Francisco earthquake was an M8.3. That number has been repeated so many times it has become an indelible part of the city's historical fabric. However, the moment magnitude—the number now used by the scientific community—was "only" M7.7, a comedown that unfortunately tends to diminish the importance of this most significant earthquake in the state's history.

2. Earthquake energy can be compared to other natural and man-made phenomena. On a moment magnitude scale, a lightning bolt is M3.2; a tornado is M4.7; the 1994 Northridge earthquake was M6.7; the 1989 Loma Prieta earthquake was M6.9; the Mount St. Helens volcanic eruption was M7.8; the world's largest recorded earthquake in Chile in 1960 was M9.5; a major hurricane is M9.6. If a meteorite with a six-mile diameter ever strikes the earth, it is expected to result in an M12.7, and that will be very exciting.

seismic waves take to travel from the earthquake source to the stations—often less than a minute, and only a few seconds for nearby quakes. This early magnitude number is the figure that the news media report right after the quake. It is always adjusted later, but it is 90% accurate and gives everyone a quick read on size and damage potential.

The instrumental computation that determines magnitude does not take into effect ground and structural conditions in the affected areas, so it cannot be used to estimate damage. An M6.7 quake far out in the desert may scare a few rabbits and rate a dozen lines in the morning newspaper; an M6.7 quake that originates below the San Fernando basin turns out to be one of the century's major disasters.

Magnitude scales came into general use in the 1950s when seismologists, the media and the public were searching for some simple device to express the size of earthquakes, that could be generated in a hurry, and could provide a common standard that several widely separated scientific observers could agree on.

The magnitude scale appears to be easy to grasp. Even though there are no upper limits on magnitudes, it is unlikely that we could have an M12.0 quake. In reality all the quakes ever reported have fallen between M1 and M10, a popular range that doesn't exceed the total number of fingers on two hands. Because of this apparent simplicity, magnitude has become the scale of public awareness. The first question always asked by media and general public alike is: "How big was it on the Richter Scale?" A quick number satisfies the need of media and the general public to relate the latest quake to previous events. There's no need to wait for any eyewitness accounts.

Alas, it's not all so simple. Magnitude is in fact a deceptively easy expression of an extremely complicated mathematical computation. The mathematical scales that are the basis for magnitude numbers are difficult to describe and understand. Also, the number can only be generated at large seismological stations with sophisticated technical capacity and personnel. There is no Do-It-Yourself Simple Magnitude Kit for home use, unless you happen to have a seismograph in your basement.

The main roadblock to general understanding of magnitude is higher mathematics. Seismographic records are converted to a number with a logarithmic scale: An increase in one whole number on the scale represents a tenfold increase in ground movement at the particular site where the seismograph is located, and an energy release 31.6 times greater. For that reason, it is incorrect to say "a magnitude 7 earthquake is 10 times more powerful than a magnitude 6 earthquake." It is much more powerful than that.

The 1994 Northridge quake caused widespread damage to concrete structures, including the parking garage at Cal State Northridge. It originated about 12 miles deep on a previously unknown reverse fault. Photo by P. W. Weigand.

An M8.0 quake releases about 1,000 times the energy of an 6.0 quake (31.6 X 31.6). Strong ground shaking of an M6 earthquake may last 30 seconds, and the shaking generated from start to finish of a long fault movement required to generate an M8.0 quake may last for three to five minutes. Energy differences escalate quickly; the amplitude of seismic waves of an 8.0 earthquake are 1,000 times as great as those of a 4.0 earthquake, and the energy released may be 10,000,000 times greater.

To complicate matters even further, more than one magnitude scale is in use. The oldest and best recognized is the Richter Scale, created by and named for Charles F. Richter, the astrophysicist/seismologist who did extensive research at California Institute of Technology. One of the pioneers in earthquake measurement and analysis, he modeled the magnitude scale after a similar scale used by astronomers to classify the brightness of stars. It uses the maximum waveforms as measured on a single type of instrument, the Wood-Anderson seismograph. Although designed for Southern California, it is applicable to central and Northern California. Despite its cosmic inspiration, the Richter Magnitude Scale only applies to earthquakes smaller than M6.0, and is often described as "local magnitude" by seismologists.

The problem is that seismographic-wave forms on the Richter Scale "saturate" or stop growing when an earth-

quake reaches a certain size. So all events above M6.0 become indistinguishable on the seismograph, even though they clearly differ in the size of the fault movement and energy released. This shortcoming led to development of other scales, just as incomprehensible to laymen but valuable to scientists. Listed here are the most common:

1. The surface-wave magnitude scale measures distant, shallow-focus quakes more accurately and provides better perspective than complex seismographic records close to the epicenter. When magnitudes are adjusted days or weeks after the event, the adjustment factors in these long-range records.

2. The moment-magnitude scale measures the length and depth of the movement area, how far rocks on opposite sides of the fault moved, and against how much resistance—a physical quantity based on the geometry of the fault plane and the total energy released. The equation is: Area of fault plane x amount of displacement x rock rigidity = Seismic Moment.

3. The energy-magnitude scale produces numbers very similar to those of moment magnitude, but involves a different computation that focuses on energy release and does not include fault-plane dimensions.

Moment magnitude is regarded by the scientific community as the most accurate expression of energy release

Intensities vary significantly from one neighborhood to the next, and accurate personal observations are the key to creating an accurate iso-seismal map (see page 70). Photo by A. E. Fritsche.

The 1952 Kern County earthquake was one of the four largest in California's recorded history, with a magnitude of 7.5 and maximum intensities of XI.

because it is a much more reliable measurement of the relative size of large quakes. Announced magnitudes of large earthquakes are nearly always based on moment-magnitude scales, but are frequently and incorrectly attributed by the media to the Richter scale.

The first magnitude numbers that are released often represent the seismographic records at only one location—U.C. Berkeley, Cal Tech in Pasadena, one of the California USGS offices, or the National Earthquake Information Center in Colorado. It may be a Richter, surface-wave, energy, or moment-magnitude number, depending on the agency. Later numbers are more sophisticated computational averages that factor in reports from stations on the Worldwide Standard Seismographic Network.

Analysis of the seismographic and field records of a large, significant earthquake can continue for several months. It is not uncommon for a magnitude to change several times; 1989 Loma Prieta was first reported in the mid-M7 range, settled down at M7.1, adjusted again to M7.0, and finally fixed at M6.9.

It turns out that different interpreters of the seismological data sometimes come up with different numbers, and scientific reports often include the "official" local, surface and moment magnitudes. Variations of plus or minus 0.2 can result from the use of different magnitude scales, dif-

ferences in the recorded P and S waves at different seismographic stations, and variations in formulas that take into account specific geologic regions.

The most practical approach for laymen is to ignore these differences, and accept the announced number as a summary "magnitude" without worrying about the scale used by seismologists—it doesn't matter outside the scientific community. Be skeptical of media reports that attempt to define the scale. If you hear a report that an earthquake was "6.8 on the Richter scale," you'll know better.

Intensity

Intensity is a measurement of the actual effects of earthquake shock waves on structures and people at specific locations. No instruments are involved; personal observations of physical effects are the determining factors.

These effects are expressed through the Modified Mercalli Intensity Scale (opposite page). While an earthquake can have only one magnitude, it will have several intensities; typically highest near the epicenter and decreasing gradually as distance increases.

Intensity reports are not issued for weeks or months after the event, because it takes that long to gather first-hand reports and assess damage to structures. Data is collected with on-site damage reports, telephone surveys

MODIFIED MERCALLI INTENSITY SCALE

Full descriptions on the Modified Mercalli Intensity Scale are quite detailed (and in some cases, old-fashioned). This simplified version helps to explain the intensities quoted elsewhere in this book. You won't be able to compute earthquake magnitude at home, but you can estimate the intensity at your specific location by comparing these descriptions to what happens around you.

I Not felt except by a very few under especially favorable circumstances.

II Felt only by a few persons indoors, especially on upper floors of buildings. A few hanging objects may swing.

III Felt quite noticeably indoors, especially on upper floors of buildings; many reports of swaying or swinging objects. Vibration similar to that of a passing truck.

IV During the day, felt indoors by many; outdoors by few. At night, some awakened from sleep. Dishes and windows rattle; walls and frames creak; liquids may be disturbed but do not spill.

V Felt by nearly everyone; many awakened. Buildings tremble throughout, with creaking of walls. A few items fall off shelves, unstable objects overturn. Trees and shrubs shake slightly.

VI Felt by all; many are frightened and take cover or run outdoors. Building damage is slight, with a few instances of fallen plaster or damaged chimneys. Heavy furniture moves; books, pictures, small items fall off shelves. Liquids splash out of open containers.

VII Damage negligible in buildings of modern design and construction; slight to moderate in well-built, older structures; considerable in poorly built or badly designed structures. Some windows and chimneys break; some cracked plaster and broken windows. Cupboard and refrigerator doors open and contents fall out. Might be felt by persons driving cars. Frequent fall of limbs and tree tops; landslides common in steep areas.

VIII People generally frightened. Damage slight to modern structures; considerable in older buildings that lack adequate bracing, with the possibility of partial collapse; great in unreinforced masonry and other poorly built structures. Chimneys, wood stoves, water tanks, monuments, solid-stone walls fall. Heavy furniture is overturned and damaged, many items fall off shelves. Water flow of springs and wells is altered.

IX Almost everyone frightened, with some panic. Damage considerable, even in well-designed structures and wood-frame houses. Ground cracks conspicuously. Underground pipes sometimes break.

X Some well-built wooden structures destroyed; most masonry and frame structures destroyed with foundations ruined; ground badly cracked. Train rails bend. Ground cracks can be several inches wide; landslides, shifts in sand and mud, wavy folds in cement and asphalt surfaces are common. Water splashes out of canals and rivers, with serious damage to unreinforced dams and embankments.

XI Few masonry structures remain standing; bridges destroyed or seriously damaged. Extensive slumping and landslides in soft ground. Underground utility lines completely out of service.

XII Total damage, and practically all buildings collapse. Lines of sight and level are distorted. Objects thrown upward into the air. Serious ground disturbances; water and channel beds seriously disturbed.

---

and written questionnaires mailed out by agencies such as the National Earthquake Information Center in Denver and the Humboldt State Earthquake Education Center in Arcata.

You can participate in this data-gathering procedure with the questionnaire on page 141. As soon as possible after you feel a quake—even if the motion is very slight—make a copy of the questionnaire, fill in the information as completely as possible, and mail it to the address indicated.

The first well-known intensity scale was developed in Europe in the 1880s by M. S. De Rossi of Italy and Francois Forel in Switzerland. It was revised in 1902 by another Italian seismologist, Giuseppe Mercalli, and then yet again in 1931 by Americans Harry Wood and Frank Neumann to include modern features such as tall buildings, motor vehicles and underground water pipes. No further revisions have been made to reflect changes in construction styles since the 1930s. Some attempts are being made to modernize the descriptions.

This Modified Mercalli Intensity Scale (MMI) is used to generate an isoseismal map, with roughly circular lines drawn through areas of equal intensity to provide a graphic "picture" of where was felt, and the damage. Generally, intensity assigned to a specific location is the typical or average effect observed there.

By reading reports in old newspapers and letters, scientists are able to compile isoseismal maps for all earthquakes where people were around to hear the trees fall, and took the time to write about it.

The Human Element

Data collected on intensities also reveal the effect of earthquakes on people, an impact that goes far beyond cold statistics. When a modest M5.7 shake centered 10 miles from your home causes your living-room furniture to sway like a ship at sea and tosses your best china across the kitchen floor, it is hard to find reassurance in the fact that the magnitude is only one-thousandth that of 1906.

Human nerves often give way faster than the weakest of buildings. Even a shock that causes a few plaster cracks and topples store fronts can send people screaming into the streets and freeze the strongest captains of industry in their office chairs.

Personal reports are notorious for their exaggerations and misconceptions; it is not uncommon for seismologists to receive letters describing huge earth waves and wildly gyrating buildings that seem to touch the ground with each giant swing. These distortions appear to be the result of both physical and mental disorientation. If a building is

The unreinforced brick chimney is rapidly becoming obsolescent in California. Bricks are subject to shearing from the sharp back-and-forth earthquake movements, and improperly installed chimneys may peel away from the house. Photo courtesy University of California EERC Library.

Damage to the Veterans Administration Hospital in Sylmar during the 1971 San Fernando earthquake presented a classic picture of older vs. modern building techniques. Center structures built in 1926 offered no resistance to the shock waves. Outer structures built in 1937 and 1947 after earthquake-resistant designs were required by building codes escaped without significant structural damage. Los Angeles Times photo.

swaying in one direction, and the observer standing on a street corner is swaying in another, then the perceived motion can be as much as twice the actual movement. While the driver of a moving car is cushioned by the vehicle's suspension system and feels nothing at all, another person seated in a chair at home will feel the floor rock and watch the walls sway and windows crack.

Mentally, the distortions may be even greater. The earth moving beneath your feet upsets your body equilibrium and affects all your senses. Small earth waves may loom as large as ocean waves rolling up the beach, as earth seems to liquefy before your eyes. Natural sounds of the quake mingle with the crash of falling dishes and the creaking of buildings until the noise seems overwhelming.

Fear is another compounding effect. Researchers indicate that this almost universal emotion is caused by both the threat of potential damage, and from the unexpected arrival of the shake—an invisible force of unpredictable strength and size, rising out of the ground. How big will it be, how long will it last? Few can remain rational when faced with these questions. To watch buildings crack and fall, water pipes burst, and roads buckle without being able to see the cause is a terrifying sensation.

Mental depression can last for some months after a big quake, caused not only by the remembrance of the actual event, and even more so by the problems involved in rebuilding and the fear that it could all happen again. There are constant reminders in the form of boarded-up buildings, torn-up streets, and the recovery of injured persons, gaps where there used to be freeway overpasses.

How Earthquakes Cause Damage

Major earthquakes can cause a broad range of damage. Most critical is the weakening, partial collapse or outright destruction of homes, commercial buildings, bridges and freeway structures. Other less-dramatic types of damage can be just as disruptive to our lives and expensive to repair.

It is always tempting to express energy in single numbers: "The 1994 Northridge quake had a magnitude of 6.7 and peak accelerations of more than 1g." However, single numbers cannot represent the complex nature of an earthquake and the damage it creates. To understand the damage caused by any recent quake, and to lessen the damage of future events, many factors must be considered.

The 1933 Long Beach earthquake did greatest damage in coastal cities where soils were unstable and residences had been constructed early in the century without regard for earthquake safety. Photo courtesy University of California EERC Library.

Strong earthquake waves make an immediate impression, but those that are long-lasting often cause the structural damage that results in injuries and fatalities.

Among the most noteworthy aspects of the 1994 Northridge earthquake were the high ground accelerations recorded in the epicental area. Photo by A E Fritsche.

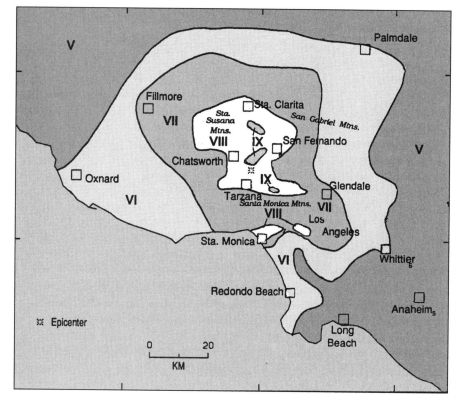

1994 NORTHRIDGE EARTHQUAKE

This is an isoseismal map of the 1994 Northridge earthquake, with reactions from various places. Most of the comments were taken from questionnaires received by the Humboldt State Education Earthquake Center in Arcata.

Northridge: "I was ready to die. I thought this was it."

"At first it felt like a wave, like you were riding on a surfboard."

Second floor of collapsed apartment house: "The whole place just fell apart. It fell and fell and then it stopped, and then I waited for the ceiling to fall on me. I never screamed because I was afraid that would be the thing that would make everything fall."

Sylmar, Herron Street: "An E-ticket (Disneyland) ride. Definitely way too much excitement."

Alder Grove Street: "The first second or so, I just thought it was another trembling, because we had one before. But then it got worse. I heard everything cracking and glass breaking and the kids screaming, it was like someone was pushing the house. I thought, if were

going to go then let the roof come down and take us—don't let us be trapped here for hours."

Fillmore: "It's like most places. These old buildings all come apart when they are shaken."

Santa Monica, 5th Street: "I stayed in bed because nothing was falling on me and I could hear crashing and breaking. I watched draperies which were violently shaking in a north-south direction. Later I noticed the TV and microwave both fell over."

Santa Monica: "It makes you feel jinxed. It drains your mental resources. After a while you feel numb."

Hollywood: "I was getting out of bed—quickly, of course. It was sheer panic. I slipped on the comforter and slid across the floor."

Hotel Guest: "It's amazing just how much worse it was on the 7th and 9th than the 5th floor. Major whiplash goes on in a tall building."

Los Angeles, Walgrove Avenue: "I'm very tired of the aftershocks and angry at Mother Nature."

Don Luis Drive: "I have lived in L.A. all my life, through the 1952 Tehachapi quake, the 1971 Sylmar, the 1987 Whittier, and the recent Landers quake. Nothing even came close to the fear I felt with this one, nor the extreme anxiety and nervousness which I felt through two weeks of aftershocks."

Selby Avenue, near UCLA: "In our neighborhood, virtually no chimneys remained intact. A mile to the north and to the south there was no visible damage."

West Los Angeles: "I've been in every earthquake in L.A. since 1964. This was the worst."

"Things were moving in both directions, up and down and crossways. I was terrified. I thought I was going to vomit. I ran to the door."

Venice, Indiana Avenue: "Apparent shaking lasted no more than about ten seconds, except for the characteristic 'house-built-on-Jell-O' gentle shaking that continued for perhaps half a minute after. I stayed centered on the mattress and rode it out. For several seconds after the major part of the quake was over, the flashing of shorting power transformers was clearly visible outside my bedroom window; multiple flashes, perhaps six or seven in the course of ten seconds or so."

Venice Blvd.: "Saw diffuse flashing light through window during shaking."
Redondo Beach—Belmont Lane: "I have felt a few earthquakes, to me this one lasted the longest. The start of this quake seemed violent, then it seemed to roll a long time after the initial shaking."

"Realized the motion was east-west because the bookcase was the only furniture to fall and kitchen cabinets didn't swing open."

Marina Del Rey, Ketch Street: "This quake felt the strongest of any since I moved here in 1984. It was also the longest."

Pacoima, Driving on I-5: "My car was weaving from lane to lane and chunks of concrete were flying in the air. All of a sudden there was a big thud and a cloud of dust. It was like an explosion. I slammed on my brakes."

Reseda, Pennsylvania Avenue: "I was in Los Angeles near LAX during the 1971 Sylmar quake, and this one felt almost identical. It seemed to last about one minute. I felt more sideways motion than up-and-down."

Van Nuys, From a student who was at UC, Berkeley at the time of the 1989 Loma Prieta quake: "It was so scary. It was so much bigger than the one in the Bay Area. I sat in the door jamb for three hours. There were so many after-shocks, I didn't feel I could move."

Sherman Oaks: "I was looking at the ceiling one moment, then I was looking out at the sky. I thought we were dead."

San Fernando Valley, Hotel guest: "In Oakland (1989) it was like one big hard bang. Today it was long and hard and wouldn't stop."

Malibu, Las Flores Canyon Road: "My whole apartment building was doing the hula."

"Cabinets and bookshelf facing east-west fell over, those facing north-south did not."

Pasadena: "The motion was fairly sharp, but not very severe. I actully thought that it was an M4.5 close by, rather than an M6.6 farther away."

South Euclid Avenue: "I am surprised at how relatively little damage occurred."

South Pasadena, Warwick Ave.: "It seemed to last a long time. I am 60 years old and it was by far the strongest and longest I have felt."

El Monte, Meadowlark Avenue: "The most annoying thing about this quake has been the constant aftershocks. They were happening all day long Monday, and I could feel them as I tried to work (Pasadena). It was distracting, and the cumulative emotional impact of hundreds of little earthquakes was much more discomfiting than the initial, large earthquake."

"As the quake was getting stronger, I thought the apartment was going to fall apart and I was going to die."

"My dog started acting funny and barked a lot."

My dog was running around the yard. I felt like my house was going to fall down. I could not stand up."

Torrance, Rolling Hills Road: "Glad to be alive! Couldn't imagine what it would be like in the epicenter."

Altadena, East Poppyfields Drive: "We're glad we've prepared for quakes but it was still pretty scary."

Marcheta Street: "Normally I stay in bed and ride them out, but this time it seemed to get stronger and longer, and the bedroom felt like it was swaying—convincing me that the poor construction job on the back bedroom would just tear it off the house and send it down the hill. That's why I got up and ran for the hall-way in the older part of the house."

Visscher Place: "We thought it was an aftershock to the Landers quake until my sister called at 5:00 a.m. to see if we were all right."

Rancho Cucamonga: "Slow building roll, no sharp movements."

Gardena: "Shake-and-twist movement as opposed to a rolling motion."

Montecito: "Clock started ticking that hadn't been wound in years."

Pismo Beach: "It lasted longer than any I've felt before. I had enough time to wake my husband, and we had time to talk about it while it was occurring."

Oceano: "Got up to go to the bathroom, felt it mildly, thought it was the train."

Anaheim, Archer Street: "Wish my wife hadn't woke me up for it."

Hotel Guest: "I'm from Japan where we have a lot of earthquakes, but I've never been in one this big. I just wanted to get up from bed, but I couldn't stand up. At first I thought, oh, just another earth-quake, then, wow, it was rough."

Hemet: "It almost threw me out of bed—not a rock-and-roller like most I've expe-rienced.

Clovis: "Motion was jarring, not rolling; pool skimmer started banging and awoke me."

Maricopa: "Mainly noticed dogs bark-ing."

Buttonwillow: "Four inches of water splashed out of the pool."

Palm Desert: "Pendulum clock stopped."

Barstow, Driving on Interstate 40, about 30 miles east of town: "Didn't feel quake; desert dirt rose five feet, settled down again, and that was it."

Calipatria: "Husband felt gentle rocking motion; I didn't feel it."

Mission Viejo: "Few cupboard doors flew open but nothing fell out."

Escondido: "Magnitude 4+ earthquakes in local mountains felt much worse than this one."

San Diego: "Our cat awakened my wife just before the quake."

"Jolting motion rather than rolling."

Campo: "It felt like a sudden jolt, like the side of the house was being hit with a battering ram; then a slight swaying movement."

Las Vegas: "Dog began pacing 10 min-utes before quake. During quake, heard windows and beams creaking and ring-ing."

Tropicana Hotel: "Chandelier swayed."

MEASURING THE MOTION

Ground motion is complex and can be expressed in several ways. The diagrams on page 29 show the variety of movements possible along different kinds of faults—right, left, up, down, and sometimes oblique—and the resulting motion is rarely easy to describe.

Displacement is the amount that the ground actually moves back and forth as the waves pass through, as expressed in centimeters or fractions of inches. One measurement taken about a mile from the fault during the M7.3 Landers earthquake in 1992 indicated a displacement of almost 24 inches. The amount of displacement can be a significant component in building damage.

Velocity is the speed of the displacement and is a critical factor in damage. Waves travel slower and have higher amplitudes in softer soils, thereby causing more damage. In downtown Los Angeles, the sedimentary layer is inordinately thick (as much as six miles). So the amount of shaking there could be significantly greater than it is on a hard-rock site; the San Fernando and San Gabriel Valleys are similar.

Acceleration defines the rate of change in velocity (how fast the ground is pushed to move), as expressed in terms of percentage of the force of gravity, or %g (a car accelerates faster when you step down hard on the accelerator, and decelerates according to how hard you step on the brake). Peak accelerations often are used as single numbers to express total ground motion, but they are only one piece of a very complicated picture. They are local measurements, are unpredictable, and vary in character. The 1983 Coalinga and 1987 Whittier Narrows events did not exhibit high accelerations; the 1992 Cape Mendocino and 1994 Northridge quakes produced some of the highest ever recorded, as much as 2g in isolated locations.

Frequency is the number of vibrations per second. High-frequency waves have high accelerations and small displacements. Low-frequency waves have low accelerations, large displacements, and high velocities.

Attenuation is the rate at which the seismic waves die off with distance, which determines the area of destruction and local intensities (see page 67). P and S waves attenuate much faster than longer surface waves that travel long distances and can damage tall buildings far from the epicenter. Waves from earthquakes in California attenuate much faster than those in other parts of the country, meaning that quakes in the mid-continent region are felt over a wider area than those of equal size in California.

Ground displacement, velocity and *acceleration* are measured on three-component seismometers. When an earthquake occurs, two of the components measure perpendicular horizontal movements, and one measures vertical movement. These measurements must always be expressed in combinations to truly reflect motion at any specific site. In the 1994 Northridge earthquake, 0.9g peak acceleration in Santa Monica was a brief, high-frequency motion that did not generate high velocities. The 0.9g peak acceleration in Sylmar was a different pulse that generated much higher velocities of almost six feet per second.

Structural Damage

Structural damage presents some of the best and worst evidence of earthquake intensities. The fact that the damage is permanent makes it ideal for detailed examination. It is not subject to personal interpretation and it remains to be studied and analyzed after the intial confusion is over.

However, such damage often tells much more about the structures themselves than it does about the earthquake. Buildings, bridges and freeway structures crack and crumble primarily because a combination of dynamic vertical and horizontal forces are exerted against structural designs meant to contend primarily with static gravitational forces. Mix these horizontal movements with a vertical component, and the structures are subjected to additional twists and turns.

Also, there often is uneven resistance in different parts of a building—a slab floor can absorb much more shock force than a large pane of glass. When the give-and-take of any structure is unbalanced, rigid, weaker elements are fractured or torn loose. The classic example is a brick chimney that cannot move with the same flexibility as a wood-frame house, and is snapped off at the roof line.

Because of its mild weather, and the architectural preferences of its residents, California has more than its share of lightly constructed buildings with large areas of glass, open ground floors, multiple towers, split levels, and highly ornamental, minimally strengthened facades. Even though light construction normally is a plus, all these complicated configurations create weak points that are susceptible to seismic waves.

Structures tied together into single units of resistance, with quality construction, stand the best chance of resisting earthquake motion. The more changes from one floor to another in the structural system of a multi-story building, the more susceptible it will be to damage. The best combination consists of shear walls, columns and other reinforcements that run continuously from foundation to roof, all tied together with well-designed and well-constructed joints.

Freeway bridges and overpasses need the same type of structural integrity. New freeways are designed with a high degree of resistance to both vertical and horizontal stresses. Retrofitting older elevated freeway structures involves strengthening both joints and columns. Steel cables are added to secure bridge sections to the support columns. Shock absorbers are inserted between the roadway and columns to lessen effects of the shaking. Hinges are used to secure roadbeds to the columns, so whole sections of the freeway can move as single units. Support columns themselves are reinforced with concrete or steel jackets to hold them together.

Building damage can result from improper design and construction, strength and duration of the shock waves, soil instability, or—most commonly—a combination of these elements. Photo by Earl Hart.

The 1992 Landers earthquake generated a series of surface ruptures on a broad belt of related faults that easily tore up roads, fences, houses and other manmade structures. Because of the arid nature of the terrain, some fissures and scarps created by this quake will be visible for years.

All things being equal, structures close to the epicenter are subject to higher risk than those some distance away. But all things are never equal. It is very common for damage to appear capricious, leveling one structure and sparing another nearby.

There are good reasons behind this selectivity. Whether a structure rides out the shock unscathed, suffers minor damage, or collapses is determined by these five factors:

1. Strength of the earthquake waves that reach the surface. Generally, the greater the magnitude, the harder the shaking, and the greater the damage potential. A weak fault movement near the earth's surface, or a giant shift far underground, cannot generate the strength required to overcome the natural built-in stability of even the weakest structures. An earthquake of M6.5 or greater, originating from a depth of less than 10 miles, will result in maximum MMI of at least VIII with some damage to structures close to the epicentral area.

Ground motion is primarily a sequence of vibrations—buildings sway from side to side in response to the waves passing through the ground beneath them. Direction of the ground motion is not related to the direction of the fault movement; seismic waves move in all directions. Horizontal strike-slip movements can produce as much vertical shaking as movements on dip-slip faults. Conversely, the strongest ground motions recorded in

recent thrust-fault earthquakes were horizontal.

In general, all earthquakes, regardless of source, produce about twice as much horizontal as vertical shaking.

2. Duration of the motion. Very rarely will an earthquake be felt as single pulse. It is a fluctuating series of tremors that last from 10 seconds to three minutes or more with duration increasing with magnitude. In big earthquakes, peak ground accelerations may be no larger than those of smaller quakes, but duration and area affected are significantly increased. Longer duration, primarily with shear waves, breaks down structural walls and is the usual cause of collapse.

Aftershocks also play an important role in the amount of damage. The main shock may weaken structures without actually knocking them down—then a relatively weak aftershock completes the destruction.

3. Proximity. This refers to the distance of a structure from the quake—including the entire fault plane where underground rupture takes place. A building can be 10 or 100 miles from the epicenter and still be on top of the earthquake, depending on the length of the fault rupture and the dip of the fault (see page 29). In most earthquakes, the surface area above the fault receives the hardest shaking, and the region within five miles will experience roughly the same motion. Beyond this, the vibration tends to attenuate rapidly, and is about half as strong beyond

Unreinforced concrete-block walls are easy prey for the horizontal earthquake movement; they topple without a struggle. This was one of dozens of similar scenes in the Granada Hills area after the 1994 Northridge quake. Earl Hart photo.

eight miles, an eighth as strong at 30 miles, and a sixteenth as strong at 50 miles. There are many exceptions, however, with complexity of the seismic waves, soil conditions and other factors affecting the amount of damage at any specific location.

Directivity of the fault break also plays a role. When the rupture moves along the fault plane, it focuses energy in the direction it is moving, so a site in "front" of the movement receives more shaking and records higher accelerations than a site the same distance from the fault, but 180 degrees away.

4. Geologic foundation. Local soil conditions are a major influence on the extent and severity of seismic ground motion and the resulting structural damage. Structures built on solid rock, even those near the epicenter, invariably fare better than those built on soft soils, unless there is an unusual energy focus created by seismic waves reflecting off underground geologic structures. Areas with heavy concentration of mud or old unengineered artificial fill (sands, quarry rubble, even garbage) that are stable under ordinary conditions turn unstable when shaken by an earthquake, and have high damage potential.

If soft soils contain porous layers of sand with high water content, the result of strong shaking can be liquefaction, whereby the sand layers turn liquid and lose their load-bearing capacity. Any heavy object on top—a build-

ing, bridge, or freeway ramp—tends to sink, often tilting and moving sideways at the same time, cracking or breaking up as it moves. When shaking stops, the soil re-solidifies and the object remains repositioned, broken and often leaning at a grotesque angle.

It isn't just aboveground structures that settle and crack; underground utility lines, especially older welded pipes that may date back to the 1920s, tend to buckle and break. Liquefaction sometimes is accompanied by sandblows, eruptions of liquefied sediments up through fissures in the ground. Observers describe them as miniature volcanoes or fountains of sand and water.

Inconsistent damage patterns result when a structure is located partly on rock or hard ground and partly on soft ground. Differential settlement imposes tremendous strain on the structure, so part may collapse while part remains unscathed.

Modern developments in foundation engineering have reduced the hazard in some types of fill; properly recompacted soils can be expected to be much more resistant to ground shaking than the loose, unstructured fills common to the 19th and early 20th centuries.

5. Structural design and construction quality. Architects and engineers continue to improve the degree in earthquake resistance in new structures, and the improvements have made a major difference. Strength is achieved by

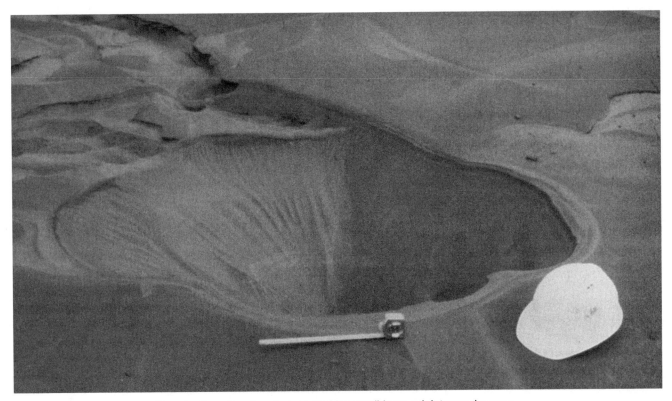

Liquefaction often is accompanied by sandblows, miniature volcanoes that spew forth liquified sediments. Photo courtesy University of California EERC Library.

adequate bracing and structural continuity, with secure anchoring and bonding of all elements—foundation, frame, outer and inner walls, upper floors and roof.

However, strength alone is not enough; a rigid "brittle" building is more susceptible to damage than a flexible one that can react as a whole to the horizontal earthquake stresses. Buildings designed and constructed before 1976 are noted for this "brittle" nature. Design also has to take into account the complicated nature of ground motion, including displacement, velocity and acceleration. Older masonry buildings are most affected by high accelerations. Damage in tall, modern buildings depends more on velocity and type of seismic waves.

Quality construction is critical, especially at connections. Weak joints in otherwise well-designed and well-built concrete-and-steel buildings sustained unexpected damage in the 1994 Northridge quake, due in part to the rotational stresses that were added to the horizontal movement.

Buildings designed and constructed since the mid-1970s have generally performed well during recent quakes. Older buildings are the most hazardous. Ordinary unreinforced masonry structures are especially vulnerable to earthquake damage because of their heavy mass and low resistance to lateral forces imposed by earthquakes. California's Unreinforced Masonry Building Law required all local governments to conduct an inventory of such buildings by January 1990, so they are now identified and their owners alerted to the danger of collapse in the next moderate quake.

Concrete-frame structures and "tilt-up" buildings with precast walls built before 1976 turned out to be vulnerable. Strengthening connection points can make significant improvements in their performance. Conventional wood-frame construction has a high degree of resistance, provided the workmanship is sound, the frame is properly bolted to the concrete foundation and walls are braced. Single-story houses of conventional design are lightweight, with multiple framing members and a degree of flexibility, ranking them among the safest structures in moderate quakes, unless there are weak joints.

Multiple-story buildings, with a "soft" first story consisting of garages, stores or large offices with lots of open space and minimal wall support, are subject to some of the worst damage. First floors typified by narrow plywood-sheathed panels, gypsum wallboard and stucco are not strong enough to resist horizontal movement of the upper parts of the building. Collapse is probable with dire consequences for people, cars, and personal property at ground level.

Buildings with large glass areas remain a problem; large windows and glass walls in homes and stores are

DIAGRAM OF DISASTER—HOW AN EARTHQUAKE WORKS

This diagram illustrates the nature of earthquake motion and the type of surface damage that can result from the shock waves. The vertical scale has been distorted to provide a clearer picture.

The movement of rocks within the earth is the starting point of an earthquake. As the rocks snap past each other, great shock waves are generated that spread out in all directions. The strength of the waves is naturally higher near the point of movement. The earthquake that causes effects such as these shown here is a big one—probably magnitude 7.0 or greater.

There are two general types of surface disturbances during an earthquake. The first is the actual rupturing of the ground that is an expression of the basic shift in the rocks.

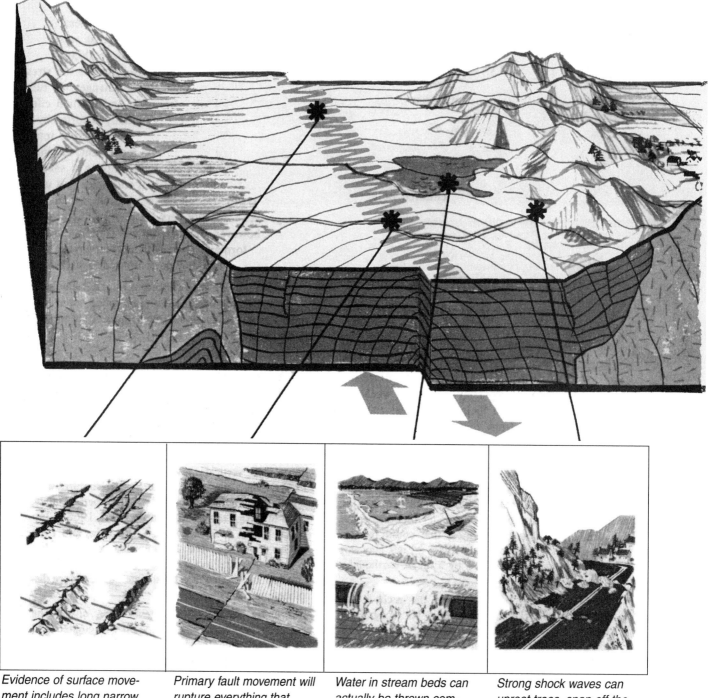

Evidence of surface movement includes long narrow ruptures, a series of parallel breaks, or pressure ridges that are "torn" in the earth. Low, steep scarps often are formed by vertical shifts.

Primary fault movement will rupture everything that crosses its path. Offsets in roads and fences often provide valuable clues in measuring the total amount of horizontal displacement.

Water in stream beds can actually be thrown completely over the banks. Shocks passing through lakes can create sizable wave fronts that splash beyond regular shore lines.

Strong shock waves can uproot trees, snap off the tops of others, and cause massive landslides. Even so, sturdy houses on solid-rock foundations may be able to survive with minor damage.

This can take place only along the fault. The second is the widespread changes in the surface that are caused by the shock waves.

The area that is affected by the shock is impossible to define. But it is not uncommon for cities 20 miles from the fault to be hard hit, and for minor damage to occur in large buildings 80 to 100 miles away.

The initial size of the earth movement and the geological structure of the earth are important factors in earthquake intensities, particularly at greater distances.

The shock waves shown here all emanate from a single point where the first fault movement takes place. In reality, other movements may also occur along the same or related faults, each creating its own shock pattern and adding to the overall concentration and duration of the surface shaking.

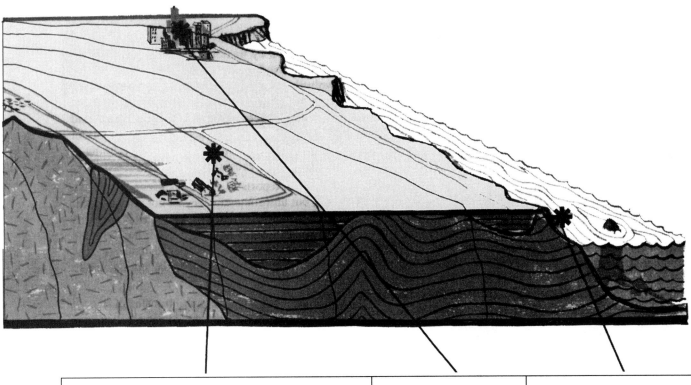

Earthquake intensities tend to be highest in alluvium and soft soils. A town located in a river basin or flat alluvial plain may be badly damaged. A similar city closer to the fault, but constructed on bedrock may escape unscathed. Large secondary slumps and lurches are common in farm areas, particularly where soil is water-laden, and are greater than primary movements on top of the fault.

At great distances, damage is usually limited to taller buildings that are swayed by slow surface waves. Damage may also occur when two buildings set up different motion and pound each other.

Along the sea coast, slumping and landslides are common steep bluffs. Underwater mud slides can destroy piers and rip cable lines. Type of soil is important in actual amount of damage done.

LESSONS FROM LOMA PRIETA

The 1989 Loma Prieta earthquake provided dramatic examples of the correlation between unstable soils and building damage:

While maximum MMI intensities were VIII in the epicentral area, they reached IX in San Francisco's South of Market District that was filled haphazardly during the city's development in the late 1800s after the Gold Rush. Some buildings settled as much as a foot. This was no surprise because this was one of the areas of maximum damage and loss of life in the 1906 earthquake.

Damage to San Francisco's Marina district was a classic example of the weak load-bearing characteristics of poorly compacted, water-saturated, fine-grained natural and artifical soils in even modest seismic circumstances. Shaking was three to four times stronger here than at Fort Mason, located on bedrock just a few blocks to the east.

The portion of the East Shore freeway that collapsed was built over filled ground; sections farther south grounded in firmer soil fared much better.

Liquefaction-related ground failure, including differential settlements, was widespread from Santa Cruz to near Salinas in areas underlain by soft, unconsolidated deposits of the San Lorenzo, Pajaro and Salinas Rivers.

Poor soil conditions in San Francisco's Marina District was the main reason heavy damage was sustained by buildings in this area. Similar buildings a few blocks away were not damaged. Mark E. Gibson photo.

often shattered. In their tightly fixed positions they are unable to withstand the twisting from complicated seismic waves. Mobile homes, unless properly anchored and braced, are as vulnerable to ground shaking as unreinforced concrete-block garden walls and bottles on a grocery-store shelf. Without any horizontal support, they fall off their foundations under mild seismic motion.

More information on prediction and prevention of building damage can be found on page 131.

Other Types of Damage

In addition to structural damage caused by shaking, other phenomena contribute to the overall damage created by an earthquake.

Surface Ruptures

A surface rupture is a "tear" in the ground directly above the fault plane, caused when by the fault movement reaches the surface. This can happen if the hypocenter was very shallow or the magnitude very significant, and usually a combination of the two. A rupture breaks or significantly offsets everything in its path, and can cause immediate changes in the landscape. They are often confused with secondary cracks and slumping frequently seen in soft soil, landslide areas and roadways. Actual surface ruptures are surprisingly uncommon.

Both the 1857 and 1906 quakes along the San Andreas fault were accompanied by surface breaks hundreds of miles long—exceptional occurrences caused by exceptional earthquakes. Lesser, still significant, ruptures were found after the quakes of 1940 in Imperial Valley (M7.1), 1952 in Kern County (M7.5), 1966 in Parkfield (M6.1), 1968 at Borrego Mountain (M6.5), 1971 in San Fernando (M6.7), 1987 in Superstition Hills (M6.6), and 1992 in Landers M7.3).

The extent of surface rupturing, if any at all, does not always correlate to magnitude. Rarely, a quake of M5.0 or less has broken the surface. The largest onshore California quake that did not rupture the surface was the M6.9 Loma Prieta in 1989, although there was extensive landsliding, slumping and secondary cracking in the Santa Cruz Mountains. Even significant fault movements sometimes cannot break the surface because of the nature of the top layer of materials. If they are loose and granular, there is nothing to fracture, and the break dies out at the upward end.

What appears to be a significant new scarp or sidehill ridge created by a surface rupture usually turns out to be insignificant by itself. Many surface features caused by

INCREASED KNOWLEDGE

Taken cumulatively, the 1971, 1989 and 1994 earthquakes added significantly to our fund of knowledge on potential structural damage. They re-emphasized these critical points:

1. Hazards of non-earthquake-resistive construction were evident in all three quakes. Old structures, particularly those characterized by unreinforced masonry bearing walls and weak mortar, performed poorly.

2. Modern high-rise construction generally survived well; however, serious questions were raised regarding certain types of concrete-and-steel buildings, particularly at welds and joints that are forced to absorb most of the earthquake stress.

3. Retrofitting of buildings and freeways can significantly reduce—but not entirely eliminate—serious damage in a major quake. Some seismologists believe that during the 1994 quake, the Golden State-Antelope Valley freeway interchange would have fallen even if it had been retrofitted to the strictest modern standards because its maximum sway was 10 feet.

4. Increased seismic-safety standards are needed for structures critical to earthquake response and emergency procedures—hospitals, utility stations, etc.

5. Greater caution is required relative to building new structures of any kind inside the known boundaries of active fault zones. Both owners and occupants should be alerted to all types of potential damage (see page 131).

6. Modern one-story wood frame and stucco dwellings did well in some situations, but failed in others. Construction quality is key to the success in the vulnerability of stucco homes and apartment houses, particularly in multi-story dwellings where the first floors consist of garages and other large open spaces with a minimum of horizontal and vertical bracing.

Structural damage from recent earthquakes, including the freeway collapses in 1994, prompted stiffer design and construction codes throughout California. K. E. Sieh photo.

DAMAGE TO TALL BUILDINGS

Certain characteristics of tall buildings make them particularly susceptible to damage from the slow and gentle rocking motion of a major earthquake as much as 100 to 200 miles away, especially if such motion includes significant displacements (see page 75).

The greatest danger arises when the frequency of the incoming seismic waves matches the natural vibration frequency of the building, a phenomenon called *resonance*. Under these circumstances the buildings begin to sway as the waves move up the building, with the greatest horizontal movement in the upper floors causing even more stress at the joints. Buildings with varying heights have different resonant frequencies. In some cases, quakes can be felt—and can cause serious damage—in tall buildings at localities where the same waves do little or no damage to poorly constructed one- and two-story structures.

Observations made as early as the 1857 earthquake (see page 89) alerted structural engineers and city planners to the problem. However, none of the California earthquakes since 1906 have produced surface waves strong enough to threaten modern skyscrapers. Tall buildings in downtown Los Angeles will be put to the test in the next M7.5-8.0 quake on the southern San Andreas Fault.

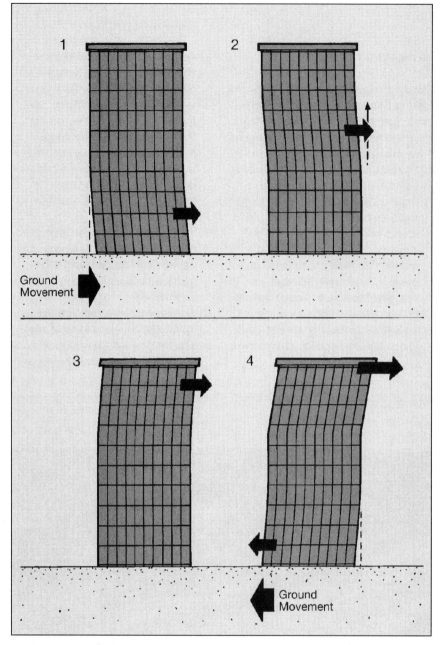

1. As the first energy waves arrive, the building foundation is pushed in one direction and horizontal movement starts upward.
2. Because floors move sequentially, upper-floor motion lags behind. Within seconds of the first displacement, the foundation moves back to its original position, starting another upward movement.
3. As two sets of waves approach the top, momentum causes upper floors to move back and forth with much greater swing than lower floors.
4. If the foundation is jolted again, complex horizontal movements put the building under intense strain.

SLOW CREEP

Sudden shifts that produce earthquakes are the most dramatic movements on faults, but another type of slower gradual movement is equally important. In some areas, opposite sides of a fault creep past each other at the rate of a quarter inch to maybe an inch or two per year. Creep is not constant; sometimes it will continue for an extended period. At other times, the movement may be measurable for a week, then stop for weeks or months. A quarter of an inch per year doesn't sound like much, but at that rate, 12 inches of offset will occur in 50 years, the life of many public buildings.

Five notable areas of creep along California's major faults are:

1. Central section of the San Andreas fault from San Juan Bautista to Cholame. One prominent location is the Cienega Winery (see page 46).
2. Calaveras fault, especially in Hollister, where offset and broken curbs and gutters are common. Numbered streets between Locust and West Streets are especially affected.
3. Southernmost segment of the San Andreas fault system, including the main trace in the Coachella Valley, the Imperial fault, and the Superstition Hills fault near the Mexican border.
4. Hayward fault (see page 43).
5. Short section of the Garlock fault near its intersection with the San Andreas fault near Frazier Park, very close to Tejon Pass.

Slow creep at the surface does not preclude the chance of a major earthquake. The fault may still be locked at depths of 2-10 miles, and capable of producing earthquakes. A major question to be answered about hidden thrust faults is whether there is any below-ground creep that could help relieve stress build-up.

All fault movement—fast or slow—is interrelated. "Instant creep" can take place during an quake, followed by a period of dormancy. Creep rates along the Hayward fault and in the Hollister area slowed noticeably after the 1989 Loma Prieta earthquake.

Fault creep is not life-threatening; the damage is repairable. Its major significance is that it shows the location of an active fault and the degree of stress building on either side. The slow movement is just another piece in the complicated California geologic puzzle. It may provide data that increases the ability to forecast future quakes.

Slow creep along the Hayward Fault in Hollister caused sidewalk to buckle upward to accommodate the compression. Earl Hart photo.

The 1989 Loma Prieta earthquake did not rupture the surface, but instances of liquifaction and secondary slumping were common. Ground slumping can cause buildings to slide down slopes and change the path of waterways. Photo by Earl Hart.

Compression of more than a foot during the 1994 Northridge earthquake caused underground water mains to crunch together and then pull apart, creating breaks that cut off the water supply. Photo by Earl Hart.

the 1857 and 1906 earthquakes have been modified by erosion or covered by landslides and other recent changes in surface contours, so only a few features are still recognizable. Scarps and cracks formed by the 1952 Kern County earthquakes were scarcely visible ten years later. The dramatic surface ruptures created by the 1992 Landers quake will last only as long as weather permits.

But nature is patient. Even though most of the features created by one quake may disappear, the accumulated displacement caused by hundreds or thousands of movements over millions of years, eventually brings indelible changes in the face of the land.

Ground Dislocations

Compaction is common during earthquakes, as soil particles settle and take up less space (look at what happens when a box of breakfast cereal is shaken). This is often seen at bridge approaches, where the roadways built on artificially constructed ramps settle when subjected to ground motion.

Another dramatic effect caused by seismic shock waves is ground compression and extension, where limited surface areas temporarily shrink by 25% or more, causing railroad tracks to buckle and bend. And underground pipes and utility lines are telescoped or torn apart. Compression in open areas creates cracks and the long, low humps called *moletracks*.

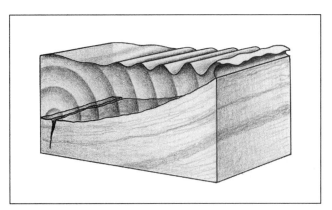

Landsliding is a universal feature of California earthquake scenarios. Very little can be done to prevent this type of damage because of the fractured nature of rocks and slopes within the fault zones. This road 10 miles east of Bakersfield, along with dozens of others, was temporarily closed by the 1952 Kern County earthquake. Photo courtesy California Division of Highways.

Tsunamis generated by major earthquakes tend to move at great speed in the open ocean—up to 500 miles per hour—but the waves generated are very low. As waves reach shallower water, the rising shoreline restricts their forward motion, slowing them to under 50 miles per hour, but increasing wave height dramatically.

Ground Water Disruption

Major adjustments in ground water are common results of strong motion. Underground dislocations of rock may interfere with the delicate system of channels that feed natural springs and wells. Water levels in wells raise or lower, water temperatures change, and old springs have been known to dry up while new ones are created nearby. At ground level, surface ruptures and secondary shifting such as landslides and slumping can reroute natural drainage systems. Earthquakes also can cause sudden alterations in geyser activity.

Landslides

Because fault zones are typified by large sections of crushed rock, and they are frequently found near the base of mountain ranges, even moderate earthquakes can cause hundreds of landslides. Roads are blocked, utility lines buried and hillside homes damaged. Surface slumping and landslides caused major damage from all earthquakes in the Santa Cruz mountains (including 1906 and 1989), and can be expected to do the same in the future. One goal of the 1990 Seismic Hazards Mapping Act (see page 127) was to identify areas most likely to experience significant landslides.

Tsunamis and Seiches

Seismic sea waves—known internationally by their Japanese name *tsunami*—are sometimes triggered by fractures along undersea faults, slumping on the ocean bottom, or a landslide in an offshore canyon large enough to start a column of water in motion.

The resulting ocean waves radiate outward in all directions at speeds that can approach 500 miles per hour. In the open ocean, the wave crests are widely separated and too low (three feet or less) to be noticed by large ships. As the tsunami enters shallow water along coastlines that may be thousands of miles from the tsunami's source, wave velocity is reduced and the height is increased. One or more such waves can break on a beach as a flood or run up a river or stream for hundreds of feet, causing considerable damage to vessels docked in harbors and to people and buildings close to the shore line. Tsunami damage can be influenced by the coastal topography (certain bays and harbors focus the energy), and generally increases with higher tide levels that facilitate the inland penetration of waves.

Tsunami size cannot be predicted from the magnitude alone; it may be large or small, depending on the ocean-floor structure as well as the direction and amount of displacement; a strike-slip earthquake that moves the sea floor horizontally cannot produce an tsunami.

RELATIONSHIPS BETWEEN MAGNITUDE AND INTENSITY

Because intensity is so dependent on the soil and structural conditions of a particular area, it may vary at two points equidistant from the epicenter, and can even change from street to street. For this reason, it is difficult to equate magnitude with anticipated intensity. These are some general estimates:

Magnitude	Intensity
1	Only measured instrumentally
2	**II**; barely felt near epicenter
4.5	**VI**; some minor damage in limited area near epicenter, felt at distances of some 30-50 miles from epicenter
6.5	**IX** or maybe X in a small area near the epicenter; moderately to seriously destructive in heavily developed areas
7.5-8	**XI-XII**; a major earthquake with surface ruptures, extensive damage and the potential for significant loss of life

This aerial photo taken Feburary 10, 1971 shows damage to a hydraulic earth-fill dam on Lower Van Norman Reservoir caused by the San Fernando earthquake. A large piece of the upstream face collapsed and fell into the water. The structure that remained standing was badly cracked. Water oozing through cracks is visible near top of photo (arrow). Fortunately, water level was several feet below normal at the time of the quake, or damage shown here would have flooded the residential area below the reservoir. A new dam has replaced this barrier. Gordon Air Photos.

Fire is a big problem after an earthquake, especially if there has been major dislocation of utilities. Broken gas lines generate dangerous fumes, falling buildings frequently cause small fires, and broken water mains hamper firefighting efforts. Photo courtesy University of California EERC Library.

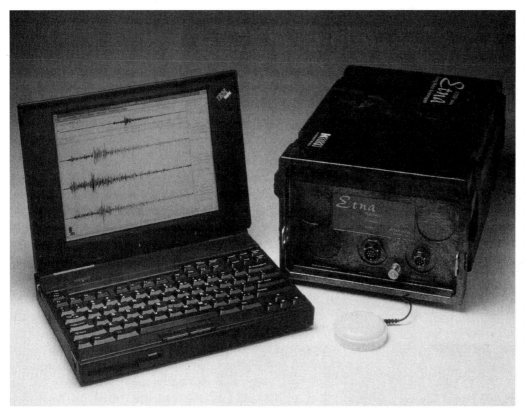

A portable seismic recorder (right) may remain in the field for as long as six months after a major quake; the Global Positioning Satellite antenna pinpoints both the location and the time of any movement recorded by the seismograph. When the recorder is returned to the lab, computers analyze the data and provide a visual representation. Seismic recorder is pictured here with a laptop computer displaying recorder output. Photo courtesy Kinemetrics Inc.

A tsunami does not consist of a single wave. It is a series, interspersed with troughs, that sometimes gives an overall effect of rapidly changing tides. In a large tsunami, the troughs can drain a harbor or offshore area for a few minutes or an hour, followed by a wave that causes a flood. On some coasts, this phenomenon is not widely recognized. Ignorance has been responsible for the death of curious observers who walk offshore during a withdrawal to observe sea life or look for treasure, only to be trapped by the next wave. A tsunami can travel great distances without losing much energy. Hawaii is vulnerable to remote-source tsunamis generated on both sides of the Pacific Ocean and even from the coast of South America.

So far, tsunamis have not been important in California's earthquakes. The April 25, 1992, Cape Mendocino quake generated a wave that caused slight damage at Crescent City and Eureka, and was strong enough to be recorded as far south as Monterey, California, and in Hawaii. An M5.2 quake originating offshore from Santa Monica on August 31, 1930, created a two-foot wave that caused one fatality and minor damage. The Santa Barbara earthquake of December 21, 1812, created a tsunami that broke along the Santa Barbara coast, reportedly carrying a ship up a canyon along the shore and then returning it to the sea on the backwash. The M7.2 Lompoc earthquake on November 4, 1927, generated a tsunami recorded locally along the California coast, and in Hawaii and Japan.

Towns along the California coast sustained significant damage from a tsunami generated by the 1964 Alaska earthquake. The tsunami reached record heights along the state's north coast and caused $10 million in damage and 11 fatalities. Crescent City sustained the most damage and greatest number of fatalities, not from the first wave, but from the third and fourth waves that surprised residents who evacuated the downtown earlier, and returned too soon in the mistaken belief that the tsunami had exhausted itself in the first surge. Other areas of significant damage included Marin County north of San Francisco and Long Beach Harbor.

Seiches, the rhythmic back-and-forth sloshing of water in harbors, reservoirs and smaller enclosed basins, can cause death and destruction if the water spills over dams into populated areas. On a much smaller scale, swimming pools can lose up to a third of their contents as the water rolls back and forth between the coping and finally crashes out in a mini-tsunami.

Fire

Fire can be the most destructive side effect of big earthquakes. Fires can develop from falling buildings, broken gas lines and overturned kitchen appliances. Many fires usually break out at the same time, and firefighters' ability to control them is often hampered by damaged highways, broken water pipes and general panic and confusion.

Unstable soil conditions, particularly along the coastal areas that were made up predominantly of loose fill, contributed substantially to the 1933 Long Beach earthquake damage.

Unstable soil problems are not unique to California; they characterized the areas of greatest damage in the January 17, 1995, earthquake in Kobe, Japan (see page 13). Akira Ono, Ashai Shimbun photo.

The fires that followed the 1906 earthquake are as storied as the shaking itself. Again in 1989, firefighters were hampered in San Francisco's Marina district because of failed water mains. Water finally was pumped to the site by fireboats in the bay.

Fire prevention should be one of the key elements in any earthquake-preparedness program for homes, offices, and schools (see page 131).

Dam Failures

However remote, the possibility of a major dam failure during an earthquake remains a significant fear in California.

There are more than 200 dams in the San Francisco Bay area alone, and hundreds more in other seismically active areas of the state. Some were built before Californians began to improve design and construction standards in the 1930s. Some have dense residential and commercial developments on the downstream sides.

So far, the only noteworthy failure was the earth-fill Sheffield Dam (since replaced) in the 1925 Santa Barbara earthquake. There was a narrow escape with partial collapse of the Lower Van Norman Reservoir Dam in the 1971 San Fernando earthquake, when 80,000 people were evacuated until the water level could be lowered.

New dams are designed and built with a high degree of earthquake resistance, and many older structures have been strengthened. The Los Angeles Dam was constructed to replace the Van Norman Reservoir embankments. Still, the fear remains; one major failure and California would have a new definition for "earthquake death and destruction."

20 Days That Shook The State
Chapter 4

The 1989 Loma Prieta earthquake created over 10 inches of horizontal movement on this 50-foot section of the San Francisco-Oakland Bay Bridge, causing connecting bolts to fail on both the upper and lower lanes. The upper section remained hinged at eastern end, so it fell into the shape of a steep ramp. Miraculously, the bridge failure itself did not result in any fatalities. The only death occurred minutes later when a confused motorist drove over the edge of the broken upper deck. Courtesy of University of California EERC Library.

Here are the top 20 California earthquakes between 1800 and 1994. Some are notable for their large magnitudes and intensities, others for their impact on the people of the state and their contributions to our knowledge of geology and seismology. Each taught us significant lessons and helped us prepare for earthquakes to come.

Descriptions vary, according to information available and the most important characteristics of each event. Comparisons are difficult. There is significant variation in the nature of earthquakes: each is unique in location, type of fault movement, intensity and damage.

Surprisingly few of these earthquakes originated on the San Andreas Fault. The most significant aspect of the 1857 and 1906 megaquakes is not that they happened, but that they are the only M7+ events to occur on the San Andreas Fault in the state's 225-year history from 1769 to 1994. For a fault as long and deep as the San Andreas, with constant slip rates of 3/4 inch to two inches per year, it is a wonder that there haven't been more M7+ events. Have we been lucky, or are the Big Ones really less common than we fear?

December 21, 1812
SANTA BARBARA
Magnitude 7.0 Maximum MMI: X

This earthquake—actually a pair of shocks 15 minutes apart—apparently centered on a submarine fault between Santa Barbara and Gaviota. It destroyed Santa Barbara Mission and Mission La Purisima near the present town of Lompoc. There was only one death, perhaps because the strength of the first shock caused people to run out of buildings that collapsed in the second earthquake.

This event is of special interest because of the tsunami that resulted. It reportedly had maximum waves of 10-12 feet at Gaviota (perhaps an exaggeration). It carried a ship from Refugio up a canyon along the shore, and then returned it to sea on the backwash.

An equally significant M7.0 quake on December 8 historically was listed as a foreshock to the December 21 event. However, recent research indicates that it originated on the San Andreas fault near Wrightwood, and was large enough to cause significant horizontal movement in that area. Shaking caused widespread damage along the entire Santa Barbara coast, including the collapse of the poorly constructed Mission San Juan Capistrano with the reported deaths of 40 Indians.

A vigorous aftershock sequence lasted through the year, making this one of the most important and long-lasting series of quakes in the first half of the 19th century.

June, 1838
SAN FRANCISCO PENINSULA
Magnitude 7.0 Maximum MMI: X

Reports of this earthquake are among the most confusing on record. Because few people were in the area at the time,

Mission Santa Barbara was badly damaged in 1812 earthquake, and then again in 1925. In both instances extensive renovation was required to restore front section and towers. Photo courtesy of University of California EERC Library.

no records provide a clue to the exact date or time. Even magnitude and location of the epicenter are uncertain. Identifying the San Andreas fault as the source may be a convenience more than anything else. This is unfortunate, because the quake was the first in a series of four significant events on the San Francisco peninsula. More reliable reports would have enabled a comparison with the 1865, 1906, and 1989 events to determine the overall long-term seismicity of this area.

The skimpy historical record is further confused by an article that appeared in a San Francisco newspaper in 1907 quoting an old-timer who claimed to have lived through a major earthquake in 1839. It was assumed that this shock was unrelated to the quake of 1838, and many early records included entries for both years. There was no other record of an 1839 quake and the confused fellow was really talking about the 1838 quake.

The most vivid personal account of the earthquake comes from the same newspaper story that reported the erroneous 1839 date. For what they're worth, these are the details:

"Mr. Brown was then living in an adobe house (behind Palo Alto near Searsville Lake) . . . He had been cutting wood and had just entered the house when he was astonished by a sudden and stunning blow on the back of the head. Looking around he saw a vat which was suspended from the ceiling, and which was used to hold lard, swing-ing about the room in a most eccentric manner. Just as he was puzzling himself to account for this remarkable phenomenon, he felt the house rock and the floor tremble beneath him. Rushing to the door he beheld a spectacle of terrible sublimity. As far as his eye could reach the earth was rising and falling in solid waves . . . the redwoods rocked like lake-side reeds. Thousands of them were broken off and hurled through the air . . .

"Mrs. Brown, at the time of the awful occurrence, was washing clothes at the side of the creek near the house. Before she was aware that the earthquake had commenced, the bed of the stream was uplifted and its water poured over her. Adobe houses . . . were cracked from top to bottom and fissures were made in their walls wide enough for a person to walk through. The ground was cracked in all directions and one immense opening was made . . . 10 or 12 feet in width, and its depth was never fathomed by man."

While these newspaper reports probably were somewhat distorted, it is apparent that this was a significant event that may have rivaled the 1906 quake in intensity along the Peninsula as far north as San Francisco. Descriptions of ground movements indicate that there was a surface rupture. Intensity levels in San Jose apparently were the same in the 1838 and 1989 quakes, and the effects in Monterey equaled those of 1838, 1906 and 1989.

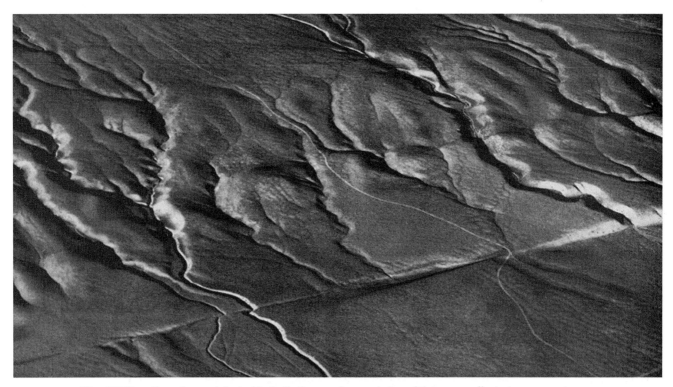

The 1857 earthquake contributed to both the number and size of the many offset streams and escarpments in Carrizo Plain. Maximum horizontal movement was over 20 feet. Note very pronounced jog in stream at left foreground. The fault can easily be followed in this northern section. John S. Shelton photo.

January 9, 1857
TEJON PASS
Magnitude: 7.8 Maximum MMI: XI

This was the strongest earthquake in Southern California's recorded history. Even though population was sparse in the areas of greatest intensity, the few available first-hand reports indicate that the shaking was as great or greater than the 1906 earthquake.

The quake occurred at 8:24 a.m., preceded by two M6.0 foreshocks thought to be centered near Parkfield. The epicenter was near Fort Tejon. The surface rupture extended more than 200 miles, with maximum horizontal displacement of 30 feet in the Carrizo Plain. Shaking lasted up to three minutes. Tremors were felt in Los Angeles, San Francisco and Sacramento. Despite its great magnitude, the earthquake caused only two known fatalities.

Most information on this earthquake comes from personal letters, military reports and scattered newspaper stories. The most detailed report of the shock appeared in a historical summary published in a Visalia newspaper in 1876 that said it was the "heaviest earthquake shock which has ever been experienced in (San Joaquin) Valley. Houses and trees vibrated violently. The solid earth seemed to have lost its stability and a wave-like motion was experienced as on shipboard . . . for a moment nature seemed filled with terror. The line of disturbing force fol-

lowed the Coast Range some 70 miles west of Visalia and thence out into the Colorado Desert. This line was marked by a fracture of the earth's surface, continuing in one uniform direction for a distance of some 200 miles."

Letters from persons in Los Angeles at the time of the earthquake tell how the tremors built up slowly in the city. Houses rocked and toppled, and people were thrown down in the streets. Because the long-period seismic waves were widely spaced at this great distance, swaying buildings had a chance to recover slightly between each successive tremor. "If the motion had been short and sudden," wrote one man, "the damage would have been appalling."

Another personal letter printed in a San Francisco newspaper included a description of surface fissures several feet wide in an area 20 miles south of Los Angeles, and of new streams of water that were created overnight. There were several reports of changes in water levels and stream courses at widely scattered points. Along the fault, the rupture created scarps and trenches. Some reports indicated breaks as much as 10 feet wide. Surface features were particularly evident in the area around Gorman and Elizabeth Lake.

At San Fernando a man reported that "the earth was in fearful agitation, with undulations so quick and rapid as to make it almost impossible to stand. The sensation was very much like that felt on the deck of a small vessel in a

The largest earthquake to occur on the Hayward fault in recorded history was in 1868. At top is a mill in Hayward that toppled completely on its side. At bottom is a private residence that suffered from both differential settling and inadequate construction that allowed its frame to separate from the foundation. Photos courtesy California Division of Mines and Geology.

heavy chopped sea." The most northerly report of surface rupture came from Cholame Valley, where a settler watched while his cabin was shaken down.

The waters of the Mokelumne River were thrown over the banks, leaving the river bed temporarily bare. The current of the Kern River was turned upstream and the water ran over the banks in four-foot waves. The water of Tulare Lake was thrown up on its shores, and the Los Angeles River was thrown out of its bed.

A U.S. Coast Survey party doing field work at Santa Barbara found long cracks in the bed of the Santa Clara River, some six to eight inches wide. Families living near the river said six-foot jets of water erupted from the cracks, and large blocks of earth sank several feet.

Reports of damage in San Francisco generally were concerned with items falling off store shelves, pendulum clocks that stopped, and a few shaken buildings.

Surface faulting from this one earthquake "freshened" many of the fault features seen in Carrizo Plain (see page 47). The lines of displacement covered an area nearly a mile wide. At one point a round corral was distorted into an S-shape by the horizontal movement.

October 8, 1865
SANTA CRUZ MOUNTAINS
Magnitude: 6.3 Maximum MMI: VIII

Reports on this, the second of four earthquakes originating on the San Francisco peninsula, are as lacking in detail as those for the 1838 event. Intensity reports indicate the epicenter was northeast of the 1989 Loma Prieta rupture, close to San Jose.

Total property loss was estimated at $500,000, with damage in towns from Napa to San Juan Bautista. Every brick building in Santa Cruz was wrecked, and ground cracking was reported throughout the Santa Cruz Mountains. In San Franciso, several poorly constructed buildings on soft soils were destroyed, City Hall was ruined, water and gas pipes were broken, and ground heaving and settling was common in the marshy area around Howard Street.

The shock was fairly strong in San Jose, where the jail and the Methodist Church were damaged. Near Santa Cruz Gap Road, chimneys were thrown down and many landslides covered the lower areas with debris. Streams near Los Gatos increased their flow, while many wells in Santa Clara County ran dry.

The 1906 earthquake could just have easily have been named for Santa Rosa, where the City Hall (above) and most other downtown buildings were destroyed. The crew here was clearing debris from collapsed main tower of the City Hall. Maximum surface rupture was in Marin County.

October 21, 1868
HAYWARD
Magnitude: 7.0 Maximum MMI: IX

At the time, this was one of the largest earthquakes in California's recorded history. It caused so much damage in both the East Bay and in San Francisco that it was referred to "the great San Francisco earthquake" until 1906. Death total was estimated at 30.

Recent research indicates that this quake resulted from a 30-mile-long fault movement that may have extended into present-day Berkeley. A 20-mile rupture opened along the Hayward fault in a straight line from San Leandro to Warm Springs (near the Santa Clara County line). The greatest damage was done at Hayward, Mission San Jose and San Leandro.

Damage in San Francisco was confined to areas underlain by unconsolidated fill; well-constructed buildings here and in other areas fared well. Most of the city felt strong tremors, however. There were reports of strange horizontal layers of dust and clean air alternating over the main business district. Passengers in a ferry off Angel Island felt the shock and thought that the steamer had run aground. Strong shaking destroyed all brick buildings in Santa Rosa, Healdsburg and Guerneville. Strong aftershocks continued into November 1868.

March 16, 1872
OWENS VALLEY
Magnitude: 7.6 Maximum MMI: XI

This, one of only four known California earthquakes of M7.5 and above, centered on the Owens Valley fault along the eastern front of the Sierra Nevada. It broke the surface for at least 100 miles from Haiwee Reservoir south of Olancha to Big Pine. Though not all reports of surface displacements agree, it appears that there were right-lateral horizontal shifts of 20-30 feet and vertical uplift of about three feet. Diaz Lake, south of Lone Pine, reportedly came into existence at this time.

About 125,000 square miles were sharply affected. It was felt from Shasta County to San Diego County and as far east as Salt Lake City. Building damage was restricted to Owens Valley; Lone Pine was virtually leveled. Severe shaking and minor damage were reported on the western slope of the Sierra and in the foothills from Visalia to Sonora. Moderate shaking was felt in the California Coast Ranges. Heavy wagons were moved by the shock waves at Camp Cady military post on the Mojave River, 140 miles from Lone Pine.

One report stated that "At the foot of the bridge southeast of Lone Pine, the disturbance in the water in the river at the time of the first shock was so severe that fish were thrown out upon the bank; and the men stopping there,

Main quad of Stanford University is less than four miles from the San Andreas fault. Its church, stone buildings and decorative arches were among the hardest-hit structures in 1906. The arch that formed the entrance to the main quadrangle was so damaged that the top section was eventually torn down. A postcard (image at bottom) shows the damaged entrance to Memorial Church. Photos courtesy Branner Library and California Division of Mines & Geology.

South of Fort Ross, the 1906 rupture snapped off tops of some redwoods and cracked others, including this 6-foot-diameter tree. The crack was 35 feet high, starting at eight inches width on this side, and tapering to a fine crack on the other side.

This one-story brick railway warehouse in San Mateo was no match for the 1906 earthquake; the wooden tower remained whole, but found itself without any support.

Contrary to the usual outward collapse of building fronts, these two-story San Francisco flats fell backward. Soon after this photo was taken, fire destroyed the entire block. Photo courtesy Bancroft Library.

The greatest horizontal movement of the 1906 earthquake, close to 20 feet, broke Sir Francis Drake Highway west of Pt. Reyes. Later photo shows highway in 1960s; the approaching car is about to cross the line of original rupture. Older photo courtesy U. S. Geological Survey.

Liquifaction of unconsolidated soils caused San Francisco buildings to settle at odd angles in the 1906; the same phenomenon occurred again in the 1989 earthquake.

The dangers of inadequate construction near fault zones were emphasized by the 1906 quake. The Thiele Building in Palo Alto (top) collapsed primarily because walls and frame were not adequately tied together. At the San Jose Hall of Justice (bottom), unreinforced stonework and heavy facings did not withstand the heavy shaking. Thiele Building photo by Richard Humphrey, Hall of Justice photo by Frank Soule.

Downtown Santa Barbara office building originally extended along two sides of a block. When it failed at the corner during the 1925 earthquake, four stories of concrete and steel came tumbling down. W. L. Huber photo. (See page 98)

Hotel Virginia had been constructed in sections over a long period. Unrelated sections swayed at different rates, smashing themselves to rubble. (See page 98)

who were engaged in building a boat, did not hesitate to capture them, and served them up for breakfast in the morning—a quite novel method of utilizing an earthquake."

The first shock lasted more than a minute and did most of the damage. Aftershocks shook Owens Valley almost continuously for several days. One report estimates 1,000 aftershocks during the first three days. The number of total fatalities is open to question; the highest estimate was only 60, primarily because of the very sparse settlement of the region.

Geologist J.D. Whitney, after whom Mt. Whitney is named, visited the site two months after the earthquake. He reported that "At Lone Pine we found ourselves in the midst of a scene of ruin and disaster . . . this town contained from 250 to 300 inhabitants, living almost exclusively in adobe houses, every one of which and one of stone--the only one of that material in the town--was entirely demolished. 23 persons killed . . . four more so badly injured that they have since died.

"At Fort Independence, which was entirely built of adobes, but in a very strong and substantial manner considering the material, the destruction was almost entire, and yet, strange to say, only one man was injured."

Owens River, 60 to 80 feet wide opposite Lone Pine, was dry along part of its course for several hours after the first heavy shock. A huge wave developed in Owens Lake. Observers first noticed the water drawn away from the shore and standing in a "wall," held by the great contrasts in currents generated in the lake. The return was gentle, so only 200 feet of new ground was covered by the waves.

April 18, 1906
SAN FRANCISCO
Magnitude 7.7 Maximum MMI: XI

Not only was this one of the greatest earthquakes ever to hit California, it also was the most significant in many other respects. Even though the 1857 quake had a larger

magnitude, it aroused very little scientific or public interest at the time because of its remote location in the sparsely populated southern part of the state. The 1906 event made the world sit up and take notice of California quakes. It provided many of the first insights into the nature of faulting and earthquakes in general, The damage it caused to man-made structures provided the basis for many building standards and rating tables still in use today.

The 1906 earthquake has become a popular event. It is frequently called the "San Francisco earthquake," because the many articles and books written about it all concentrated on the tragic destruction of the city by the combination of earthquake and fire. However, the area affected by the quake extended far beyond the limits of San Francisco, from Humboldt County to San Juan Bautista. Maximum intensities were reported in Santa Rosa, at Stanford University, and in San Jose as well as sites within the rupture zone. Many of the University's largest buildings and landmarks were shaken down by the quake. Most other towns on the east side of the San Francisco Peninsula were also roughed up to some degree, particularly San Mateo and Palo Alto. Agnew State Hospital was smashed to rubble. More than 100 persons were killed.

In terms of lost lives and property damage, this ranks as the first of the great California earthquake disasters. Death toll was reported at more than 600, with property loss estimated at $400 million. Recent historical research indicates that to minimize the bad publicity and to rebuild the city as fast as possible, the severity of the earthquake, and the damage and deaths it caused was deliberately understated at the time. Loss of life over the entire affected area probably was in the thousands. Photographs indicate that much of the damage blamed on the fire actually resulted from very intense ground motion.

The main 5:13 a.m. quake probably originated offshore near San Francisco, and created 45 to 60 seconds of intense shaking. It was preceded by a strong foreshock a minute earlier. The surface ruptured for more than 250 miles,

In 1925, stone walls at the Unitarian Church in Santa Barbara failed and the entire front section crashed down. Unstable ground conditions contributed substantially to damage throughout the downtown area. (See page 98)

from the Mendocino coast to San Juan Bautista, a break equaled only by the 1857 Fort Tejon earthquake. The nature of the rupture varied, with the greatest offset in Marin County near Olema and much smaller displacements of less than five feet near the southern end of the rupture zone.

Horizontal displacements of 15 to 20 feet astounded the scientists of the time, who had assumed that fault movements were predominantly vertical. This new evidence pointed to such a drastic departure from previous thought that the official publications of the earthquake tended to hedge on reports of long-term horizontal movements. It was even thought for some time that the 1906 fault movement was an exceptional event. Today, it is well known that most of the major faults around the circum-Pacific basin and elsewhere are capable of similar horizontal shifts.

The significance of the San Andreas fault became fully recognized with this quake. A State Earthquake Investigation Commission, headed by geologist Andrew Lawson of the University of California, was appointed to study the event. The commission's report, published by the Carnegie Institution of Washington, is the greatest report of its kind ever published on an earthquake. Its pages are still referred to by any geologist who wants to study the 1906 earthquake in particular, and faulting in general.

The elastic-rebound theory that forms the basis for current ideas on earthquake movement was first stated as part of the Earthquake Commission Report. Geologist H.F. Reid examined the 1906 evidence, re-evaluated triangular survey data gathered between 1851 and 1892, and then formulated the idea that strain built up within the rocks and then was released as energy when these rocks "snap" back to an unstrained position. The theory has since been modified and improved (see page 57); however, the basic ideas are still the same as those presented by Reid. The U.S. Coast and Geodetic Survey triangulation networks that had gathered the first evidence of elastic build-up of stress were given great impetus by the 1906 earthquake. It was realized that measurements of this type might hold the key to answering many questions about the nature of quakes.

Damage to man-made structures in 1906 clearly indicated the influence that soft sediments and filled areas can have on earthquake intensity. In San Francisco, buildings on fill were hardest hit, while structures on top of rocky hills sustained only slight damage. This evidence was further strengthened by the damage done at Santa Rosa, located in a flat alluvial plain—the type of ground associated with the highest earthquake intensities. The combination of poor ground and poor construction produced unusually severe damage for a site 20 miles away from the fault.

The State Earthquake Commission report includes hundreds of personal reports of earthquake effects and damage, and represents the first organized attempt to use such observations to create a very accurate picture of the

1933 earthquake buckled walls of Methodist Episcopal Church in Compton, causing roof to fall into the building. "The Rock" was the title of a biblical drama originally scheduled for that day.

This wood-frame residence was damaged in 1933 because of dissimilar structural materials, inadequate lateral reinforcement, and lack of strong ties between walls and the foundation. Stucco structure next door did not suffer the same problems. W. L. Huber photo.

strength and range of the shock waves. Because of the early hour of the earthquake (5:13 a.m.) many reports from rural areas were concerned with observations made while milking cows and doing other morning chores. The amount of milk spillage out of shallow pans was the subject of innumerable comments; this reporting reached its finest point at Templeton in the Salinas Valley, where it was observed that "skimmed milk was spilt at one place but unskimmed milk was not."

Within San Francisco, it was difficult to separate earthquake and fire damage. Dozens of fires broke out even while the final shudders were dying away, and the flames quickly swept through many of the areas hardest hit by the earthquake. Sagging buildings were demolished before the extent of their damage could be recorded.

June 29, 1925
SANTA BARBARA
Magnitude: 6.3 Maximum MMI: IX

This earthquake originated on an marine extension of the Mesa fault or on some other unknown fault. Almost the entire business district of Santa Barbara—including all buildings constructed on loose fill—was destroyed. Nearby cities of Goleta and Naples were hard hit and the dam at the large Sheffield Reservoir on the Santa Ynez fault north of the city collapsed. Total property damage was estimated at more than $8 million. There were about 13 deaths.

Among the most conspicuous failures were major hotels and office buildings, the courthouse, jail, library, churches and especially schools. The result was an awakening of public concern over the unstable soils, poor design and shoddy building practices that characterized sites of the worst destruction. Well-constructed buildings and those on solid ground or pavement held up very well. A reform movement was born that would grow steadily and reach a peak after the 1933 Long Beach earthquake.

Santa Barbara and Goleta residents reported that just before the main quake, a heavy rumbling sound, similar to thunder, seemed to come from the ground. There were many more aftershocks than expected from a quake of this size, with five of significant magnitude in July alone. See photos on pages 96-97.

March 10, 1933
LONG BEACH
Magnitude 6.2 Maximum MMI: IX

This quake, like that of Santa Barbara in 1925, had long-term effects well out of proportion to its modest magnitude. Because it occurred in a highly developed area of southern California, where heavy concentrations of commercial buildings and private residences were located on poor ground, it turned out to be one of the major earthquake disasters in the state's history.

In fact, this was southern California's most-talked-about quake until the 1971 San Fernando shake that out-

The most alarming damage in the Long Beach area was to public schools. Many buildings, including Jefferson Junior High School (top) and Compton Union High School (bottom), offered little resistance to the shock waves. Fortunately, the main quake struck late in the afternoon when schools were empty. Resulting investigations resulted in passage of the important Field Act (see page 127). Photo Jefferson School courtesy U.S. Coast and Geodetic Survey. Compton photo by W. L. Huber.

did the Long Beach event in property damage and relegated it to secondary status in the minds of residents.

Despite its recent demotion, the 1933 quake still rates attention for the lessons it taught Californians and for its legislative impact. The epicenter was offshore, three miles southwest of Newport Beach, on the southern segment of the Newport-Inglewood fault. This earthquake ended forever the unfounded claims that the Los Angeles was free of danger from major earthquakes from faults under and around the basin. There were 115 fatalities and damage exceeded $40 million. Both numbers are far out of proportion to the size of the earthquake.

The greatest damage was in the coastal cities—particularly Long Beach—where many public buildings, including schools, were constructed on fill or water-soaked alluvium and sand. The main quake came at 5:54 p.m. Had it occurred three or four hours earlier when classes were in session, the casualty list would have been much longer. Public outcry against inadequate design and construction techniques now reached a crescendo and the Field Act that mandated construction standards for schools throughout the state, was the result.

This earthquake also presented a classic example of panic and the spread of rumor during and immediately after a major shock. One popular story was that the Catalina Channel had sunk 369 feet and that was 30 feet of horizontal movement along the fault. In reality, there was no movement in either case.

The effects of the earthquake were bad enough without

distortion. "It seemed that the highway was coming toward me in waves and the automobile became unmanageable," one man stated. "Other cars zigzagged in the road. Tall ornamental light standards along Anaheim began breaking off and showering the car with debris. I continued along toward Long Beach and had almost reached a tank farm when a series of gas tanks exploded. A transformer station went out at almost the same time, with a dazzling pyrotechnic display."

May 18, 1940
IMPERIAL VALLEY
Magnitude 7.1 Maximum MM Intensity: X

If the 1925 and 1933 earthquakes alerted Californians to the dangers of poorly constructed buildings, this quake provided engineers with the first records of strong earthquake motions that would become a baseline for future design and construction standards. This earthquake exposed the exact line of the Imperial fault. The epicenter was at the northern end of the fault, east of El Centro. Ground ruptured for 40 miles from Imperial to Volcano Lake in Baja California. There were nine deaths, with property loss in excess of $5 million. Eighty percent of the buildings at Imperial were destroyed; 50 percent of Brawley's structures were severely shaken. Indirect damage to crops was substantial, because of disruptions of drainage channels and flooding after the break.

The main shock took place at 8:36 p.m. Residents in the

The 1940 earthquake was noted for its significant horizontal movement—30 inches here on the El Centro-Holtville Highway and as much as 19 feet in the farmlands—and for its surface rupture. F. N. Brune photo.

affected area reported 10 to 15 seconds of shaking. An M5.5 aftershock at 9:51 p.m. did most of the damage at Brawley. There were dozens of other aftershocks during the next four days. Loss of life was very low in relation to structural failure.

The maximum horizontal displacement—19 feet—was eight miles east of Calexico. The completed, as yet unfilled, International Canal was offset 14 feet, 10 inches, creating a permanent change in the U.S.-Mexico boundary line. State Highway 98, eight miles east of Calexico, was broken by a four-foot scarp, and rows of trees in an orange grove south of the highway and west of the Alamo River bridge were offset almost 10 feet. Baja California experienced some flooding.

Considerable damage was reported in Mexico and Arizona. The Yuma Weather Bureau reported that ". . . in the lower Yuma Valley, cracks opened up in fields and water and sand gushed up; wells spouted as much as 15 feet into the air; ground levels were so affected that some fields will have to be releveled."

This quake was large enough to relieve stress throughout what is called the Brawley Seismic Zone that includes the southeastern end of the San Andreas fault and the northwestern end of the Imperial fault. Quake frequency dropped significantly until the mid-1970s, when the normal historical pattern resumed.

July 21, 1952
KERN COUNTY
Magnitude 7.5 Maximum MMI: XI

One of the four highest magnitudes ever recorded in California, this was the largest in Southern California since 1857. The geological significance of the quake is even greater, because it was the first in a series of events that revealed the nature of hidden thrust faults.

Of the four historic California quakes of M7.5 or higher, this one was unique in the length of the surface break, only 17 miles between Arvin and Caliente. The source was the White Wolf fault, originally thought to be a very short strike-slip fault, traceable for less than 40 miles between State Highways 58 and 99 south of Arvin. This very large earthquake on what was assumed to be a very small fault was puzzling, because fault size is a prime factor in the size of quakes it can generate. So was the motion—left-lateral, with a significant reverse-slip component.

Now, with data from the 1971, 1978, and 1994 earthquakes at hand, geologists realize that the surface rupture was a very small representation of a large, previously unrecognized thrust fault. Even though the below-ground movement totaled about 45 miles, the quake was large enough to break the surface only in a limited area.

Shaking hard enough to be felt over an area of some 160,000 square miles awakened people throughout the southern part of the state. Water splashed out of pools and tanks in San Francisco and Los Angeles.

Because of the general low-density population of the area and the early hour (4:52 a.m., PDT), there were only

Old buildings in Brawley and other towns in the Imperial Valley could not withstand the combined effect of the main 1940 shock, plus the strong aftershock 90 minutes later. Photo courtesy of U.S. Bureau of Reclamation.

12 deaths with 10 of those in Tehachapi. Maximum intensity was confined to a small area southeast of Bealville. Tehachapi and Arvin suffered heavy structural damage, mostly confined to older brick and adobe buildings that were not adequately reinforced. Most commercial buildings and wood-frame houses designed and built since the 1933 Long Beach earthquake withstood the shocks with very little damage. Large earth cracks and landslides occurred over a considerable area, as did changes in the flow of creeks, wells and springs. Caliente Creek was dry at the town of Caliente before the earthquake; a few days after the shock, its flow was 25 cubic feet per second.

Agricultural losses ran into millions of dollars in the Arvin-Wheeler Ridge area because irrigation systems failed and crops were lost. Near Bealville, where the fault crosses the Southern Pacific Railroad, four tunnels were destroyed and rails were twisted and buckled. A crustal shortening of 10 feet was measured in one area and reinforced-concrete walls up to 20 feet thick were cracked.

Several-hundred aftershocks were recorded over a period of months; more than 20 had a magnitude of five or greater, and six occurred on July 21. The most severe came a month later, on August 22, with a magnitude of 5.8. The epicenter was close to Bakersfield and the intensities in that town were greater than those of the July 21 shock, resulting in two more deaths and millions of dollars of additional property damage.

The average number of quakes decreased throughout Southern California after 1952, suggesting that this one event relieved regional tectonic stress over a large area.

February 9, 1971
SAN FERNANDO
Magnitude: 6.7 Maximum MMI: XI

Although this was the strongest quake to strike the greater Los Angeles area in 50 years, it was not a super quake in terms of magnitude. It affected a heavily populated area, causing 65 deaths and about $500 million in property damage.

This was the first quake to produce an exceptional number of valuable instrumental records of movement on a reverse fault near a very populous area. Ground motion was significant for its high accelerations—in the 0.5 to 0.75g range, with peaks in excess of 1g. The strongest motion lasted only 10 seconds, still long enough to cause damage greater than anticipated from an M6.7 quake. Modern high-rise buildings in areas of moderate shaking performed well, but some failed in the area of heaviest shaking.

The first shock came at just 40 seconds past 6 a.m., a second shock of M5.4 came at 6:01 a.m. and another four aftershocks hit within the next few minutes. The source was on the reverse faults beneath the southern margin of the San Gabriel Mountains, on an unrecognized extension of the San Fernando branch of the Sierra Madre fault zone, about 10 miles north of San Fernando and seven miles east of Newhall. Initial displacement was about eight miles deep. The break continued upward and southward on a slanting plane and reached the surface in the Sylmar-San Fernando area.

Force from the 1940 earthquake threatened to throw down this brick column in Brawley, but the weight of the roof provided just enough pressure to hold it in place.

The surface ruptured erratically for about 10 miles (from the San Diego Freeway to Big Tujunga Canyon). The fractures were very complicated, spreading over a area several hundred feet wide at some points.

In the Sylmar area, breaks occurred right in the middle of a residential area, causing the collapse of houses, rumpling of sidewalks and extensive damage to utility lines. The communities of Pacoima, San Fernando, and Sylmar sustained the most damage. The greatest loss of life was at the Veterans Hospital in Sylmar, where the collapse of old buildings resulted in 45 deaths. Overall, it is estimated that 80 percent of the industrial and commercial firms in the San Fernando Valley sustained some damage.

In addition to the Veterans Hospital, other structures that sustained major damage included the Olive View Hospital, the Sylmar electrical switching and rectifying station of Pacific Intertie, the San Fernando juvenile facility, Pacoima Lutheran Hospital, Holy Cross Hospital, and Indian Hills Medical Center.

Among the most fascinating instances of ground motion came from the Los Angeles County Fire Station at 12587 North Dexter Road in San Fernando. At the time of the quake a 20-ton firetruck was parked inside the station, in gear and with the brakes set. When the shaking was over, firemen found the truck had moved 6 to 8 feet without leaving any visible skid marks on the floor. In addition, marks on a door frame three feet above the floor

Tehachapi's huge water tank (background) was wrenched down by the 1952 quake, sending a wall of water rushing down the street that wrapped one car around a telephone pole and crumpled another. Photo by Edwin A. Verner.

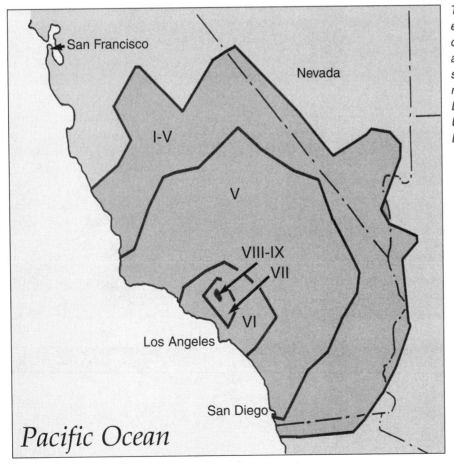

The 1971 San Fernando earthquake shook up most of southern California. For an explanation of the intensities expressed in Roman numerals, see page 67. Diagram courtesy of University of California EERC Library.

Among the elevated freeway structures damaged in 1971 was the Highway 5 and 210 interchange. Structural engineers were dismayed at the extent of freeway damage. Immediate steps were taken to strengthen highways throughout the Los Angeles area. Robert E. Wallace photo.

Landsliding caused significant lateral and vertical displacement to railroad tracks as well as highway bridge approaches and highways in the mountains. Los Angeles Times photo.

The 1971 quake overturned heavy equipment at the Sylmar electrical converter station. Extensive damage was experienced on telephone, power, gas, water and sewer systems throughout northern San Fernando Valley. T. L. Youd photo.

Large expanses of glass were snapped out of their frames or fractured in the 1971 quake, even in buildings that remained standing with very little other damage. Photo courtesy of Cal State Northridge.

At Olive View Hospital, major damage was to the carport (right), three multi-story stairway units, and a two-story portion of the recently constructed building. Carport was only one story; the reinforced concrete roof slab was supported on columns without walls. When columns failed at the top, several vehicles were crushed. Robert E. Wallace photos.

were apparently caused when the truck hit the frame. If this evidence was interpreted correctly, then ground motion surpassed 1g at this particular point.

A potentially disastrous situation developed when the earth-fill dam on Lower Van Norman Lake failed under the intense shaking, and a large piece slid into the reservoir. (see photo on page 84). Fortunately, the remaining section of dam held until the water level could be lowered to alleviate the danger. There were more than 1,000 landslides in the foothills to the east and the San Gabriel mountains to the north, but they were not a major cause of damage.

In the downtown area of Los Angeles, about 30 miles from the epicenter, 675 buildings were reported to have major structural damage, and another 900 sustained moderate damage. A dozen freeway overpasses in the northern part of the San Fernando Valley were damaged, with temporary closures of portions of the Golden State, Antelope Valley, Foothill, and San Diego freeways. Data from these failures was valuable in initiating the state's freeway-retrofit program.

Generally, the aftershock pattern was quite normal, both in number and strength. There were about 200 quakes of M3.0 or greater through March 1; an M4.6 aftershock on March 31 was centered in Granada Hills.

November 8, 1980
HUMBOLDT COUNTY
Magnitude 7.2 Maximum MMI: VII

This largest quake in California in the 1980s caused only $3 million in damage because of its remote location.

However, it was significant because it renewed attention to the seismicity of the North Coast, and clearly indicated that the offshore Gorda Plate generates significant intraplate earthquakes (the most recent was an M5.4 event on December 26, 1994).

The well-defined aftershock pattern revealed that the quake was caused by a 60-mile-long, left-lateral strike-slip movement on a fault offshore from Humboldt County. The epicenter was about 40 miles northwest of Eureka. Intense shaking started at 2:27 a.m. and lasted 15 to 30 seconds. Damage to man-made structures in Humboldt County was slight, and spectacular in one instance as the southbound lanes of U.S. 101 at the Tompkins Hill overpass south of Eureka collapsed. Six people were injured in two separate accidents caused by the bridge collapse.

In the small towns around Eureka, a few older chimneys fell and windows shattered; few buildings collapsed. In Fields Landing south of Eureka, numerous cracks appeared in roads and parking lots, and similar secondary ground surface failures were reported, including landslides and slumping along the Eel River and at Big Lagoon.

Of greater interest were the aquatic effects. There were several reports of a glow on the ocean horizon during the quake; some scientists speculated that the phosphorescent plankton common to these ocean waters were lighted up by the vibration. Fishermen who used sonic depth finders to locate fish reported that an offshore trench west of the Klamath River deepened by at least 10 feet. There was no tsunami (see page 80), but there was a very large submarine landslide off the mouth of the Klamath River.

The greatest loss of life in the San Fernando quake was at Veterans Administration Hospital at Sylmar; the death toll of 45 would have been higher had quake struck during normal business hours. Los Angeles Times photo.

Porches and decks not solidly tied to residences quickly collapsed when subjected to earthquake motions, bringing down outer house walls and inadequately supported roofs. U.S. Geological Survey photo.

May 2, 1983
COALINGA
Magnitude 6.5 Maximum MMI: VIII

The movement that caused this locally disastrous quake was on a previously unmapped 20-mile-long thrust fault; with the epicenter nine miles northeast of Coalinga. It was equal in importance to the 1952 Kern County quake in the understanding of hidden thrust faults. At the time, it was thought that the size of the quake was surprisingly large for such a short fault. Later comparison with those of 1952, 1971 and 1994 shows that it was not a unique, or even unusual, thrust-fault earthquake.

The rupture area and ground motion were complex; shaking lasted about 30 seconds. There was no surface rupture; later investigation showed the fault was marked by surface folds known as the *Coalinga anticline*. The Kettleman Hills that grew as a result of the same compressional forces that caused the earthquake turned out to be the most significant news of all.

The initial shock at 4:42 p.m. was felt from Susanville to Los Angeles and into western Nevada. A large aftershock a few minutes later contributed to the damage total by bringing down buildings damaged by the initial ground motion. There were more than 200 injuries. Property damage estimates were more than $10 million.

Heavy ground shaking rather than surface cracking or liquefaction caused the destruction of old, unreinforced masonry buildings in Coalinga and Avenal. The worst effects were in the downtown commercial district of Coalinga, where 59 of 139 buildings collapsed or were heavily damaged. Old one- and two-story buildings of unreinforced brick-masonry-wall construction, with floors and roofs of wood, fared very badly. Public buildings, and commercial buildings with walls of reinforced concrete blocks or prefabricated metal, stood up well. The majority of the injuries occurred in older residential sections where many single-family houses did not meet modern construction standards.

The aftershock pattern was interesting. In the first 24 hours after the main shock, there were 61 aftershocks of M3.0 or greater. An M5.2 aftershock on June 11 caused a small surface rupture on the previously unnamed Nunez Canyon fault northwest of Coalinga. Thousands of other aftershocks were highlighted by an M5.3 on July 9 and an M6.0 on July 22.

Coalinga is only 20 miles from Parkfield. There is some conjecture that this earthquake series, plus a few other small quakes in the area, relieved enough stress on the central section of the San Andreas fault to change the normal earthquake frequency, thus delaying the Parkfield quake that was expected between 1987 and 1993 (see page 47).

The 1983 earthquake did its greatest damage in downtown Coalinga. Almost half of the buildings were constructed before earthquake standards became part of building codes. Most of these were lost, while well-engineered structures held up well. U.S. Geological Survey photo.

Three cars parked on Coalinga's main street were crushed as unreinforced brick facings peeled off commercial buildings. Photo courtesy University of California EERC Library.

MYTHS AND REALITY

Every major earthquake is followed by assorted stories of strange happenings and unbelievable sights. Some of the anecdotes turn out to be true. Most are exaggerations caused by the inevitable panic and disorientation that accompany the quake, or outright falsehoods based on myth and speculation. These are some of the most common phenomena.

Earthquake Weather

Many residents of Earthquake Country are convinced that a definite set of conditions are part of a pre-quake scenario—earthquake weather. In Northern California, it is hot, humid, windless days, scarcely a leaf blowing—the quiet before the storm. In Southern California, it may be the days when the Santa Ana winds blow in from the desert, with high temperatures and low humidity. Most often, it is the type of weather you personally associate with the last big earthquake in your memory.

However, there's little statistical data to indicate that any type of weather has an effect on the occurrence or non-occurrence of earthquakes. Earthquakes start several miles beneath the surface; warming and cooling effects of weather cannot penetrate the earth more than a few feet. The chart on page 10 shows the earthquake pattern by month since 1800.

Months with the warmest weather—August and September—have not had a single quake of M6.5 or larger since 1800. However, the same chart does lend some support to one theory about weather. Limited research indicates that the number of earthquakes in California may increase in the fall months when large air masses associated with rain are on the move. It turns out that 16 of the 45 listed quakes (35%) occurred between October 15 and December 31.

As air fronts shift and barometric pressure drops, total air pressure at the earth's surface increases by thousands of pounds. If enough underground stress has already accumulated along a fault, then this increased barometric pressure might be enough to "trigger" a fault movement (see page 121). This is a questionable conclusion to draw from the limited data available, and a few hundred more years of records definitely are needed.

The origin of the term earthquake weather lies with Aristotle, who taught that earthquakes were caused by winds imprisoned in underground caverns that shook the earth as they tried to escape. Therefore, earthquakes occurred on windless days, when breezes were trapped in caverns. This association with escaping winds and gasses was very popular with early scientists and the idea was perpetuated for many centuries. Even today the idea's popularity is probably due to its repetition in ancient literature.

Animal Actions

If an earthquake is troubling and mysterious to humans, it is doubly so to animals. Dogs, cats, horses, and birds notice small foreshocks, sense changes in electrical or magnetic fields, or feel the first P waves before humans do. They react quickly and frantically. Animals run in circles and make strange, frightened sounds. Flocks of birds rise into the air as one. When the shaking stops, the animals and birds tend to be fearful of the spots where they were sitting or standing when the earthquake struck. They continue their erratic behavior.

Such simple and normal reactions lead to strange stories about the mysterious sixth sense of animals that warns them of impending doom. In reality, the reactions are completely in harmony with the animals' sharp senses, general fear of the unknown, and tendency to act according to instinct.

Fish suffer a unique fate because they have nowhere to go to escape the shock waves that differ little from those caused by a major underwater explosion. They often die by the hundreds.

Earth Fissures

Even though surface ruptures and secondary slumping are very real earthquake phenomena, fissures that open and close like the jaws of death are not. Treatment given earthquakes in some literary fiction and movies features huge

Scenes such as these can cause long-lasting depression; those who have lived through the quake often face months of rebuilding, always fearful that they may go through another shake-up at any time.

cracks that open up, swallow people and buildings, and then snap shut. This is untrue. Cracks may open in the ground, and there may even be an momentary opening and closing of the earth, but on a very small scale.

No one in California has ever dropped from sight into an earthquake fissure. In 1906, a cow was supposedly killed when it fell into a crack that opened on a ranch in Marin County. It is more likely that the animal fell into one of the trenches commonly formed when a great earthquake ruptures the surface, or was killed during the shaking and buried in a trench by its owner (see page 40).

Earth Waves

One of the more frightening earthquake phenomena is the appearance of earth waves, similar to ocean swells, that race across the ground. These are most often seen in areas of considerable loose alluvium or fill. Most reports of "huge" waves include a note of surprise that they did not rupture the ground. There is good reason—ground waves are not as large as they seem.

Ground waves definitely do occur. Often, observations of small waves are complicated by panic and loss of equilibrium of the observer as well as by air-pressure changes just above the ground. So perception is much greater than reality. Waves of six inches to one foot are not uncommon in large earth-quakes; reports of four- or six-foot crests are probably not believable.

Mysterious Lights

Records of great earthquakes include hundreds of reports of strange lights seen as the earth begins to shake. At one time, these lights, described as "flashing" or "streaks of lightning," were thought to be part of pre-event sequence that could signal the impending arrival of an earthquake.

Reports became so persistent in early 20th Century quakes, even in clear daylight hours, that there was a serious attempt to identify the sources. Where earthquakes occur in heavily populated areas, seismologists trace many of the "strange lights" to electrical shorts and arcs.

But there are reports of lights that cannot be explained by weather or electricity. One theory relates the lights with static electricity, perhaps caused as large rock formations shift and scrape by each other. However, more evidence and accurate observations are needed to reach any conclusions. The important point is that the lights are earthquake effects and have nothing to do with causes.

Loud Sounds

Reports of earthquake sounds are very common. They do not always agree, because there are so many possible sources of natural and man-made noise—snapping tree limbs, landslides, creaking buildings, breaking glass.

There is a definite earthquake sound that is quite separate from the rattling of dishes and the cracking of walls. It is often described as a low-pitched moan or roar that is best heard in quiet, rural areas that lack the cultural noise of city life. The sound is caused when some of the seismic P waves (see page 62) are transmitted into the air as sound waves that are sometimes audible to people, and more often to animals.

Under the right conditions people "hear" the P waves, and then "feel" the larger S waves that arrive a few seconds later. The sound tends to be sporadic and short-lived and gains much of its mysterious quality from the inability of the listener to pinpoint its origin.

During large quakes, the noise can be quite loud and becomes mixed with all the other attendant sounds. Reports often depend on local conditions:

1872, Owens Valley: "Some described the noise as resembling that made by a whole park of artillery, shot off in rapid succession, with the rattling of musketry between."

1933, Long Beach: "A low rumbling noise resembling a heavy truck passing on the street."

1957, Daly City: "I thought it was a jet plane."

Experience during the quakes of the 1980s and 1990s have provided enough data to enable engineers to identify buildings most likely to be damaged in future quakes because of their inadequate design and construction. Photo courtesy University of California EERC Library.

As with previous earthquakes, the 1987 Whittier Narrows quake quickly exposed problems of buildings built before 1933, in Whittier (top) and Pasadena (bottom). Pasadena photo by Chris Wills. Whittier photo by Los Angeles County Fire Department.

Columns in parking garage at Quad Shopping center cracked during the first quake; a large aftershock three days later caused most of the garage to cave downward. Photo courtesy University of California EERC Library.

October 1, 1987
WHITTIER NARROWS
Magnitude 6.1 Maximum MMI: VIII

While not significant for its magnitude, this quake was noteworthy for two reasons:

1. It originated on a previously unidentified thrust fault beneath the uplifted Puente Hills and Elysian Park-Montebello Hills; the epicenter was 12 miles east of downtown Los Angeles. This event, only 16 years after the San Fernando quake, provided more evidence to residents of the Los Angeles basin that their greatest danger might not come from a massive earthquake on the San Andreas fault, some 50 miles away. More frequent midsize quakes generated on smaller, often unrecognized, thrust faults very close to population centers were possibly a greater threat—a prophecy borne out in 1994. There was no surface rupture, but secondary slumping and ground cracks were common.

2. It caused the second-highest dollar damage amount of any California quake in the 1980s—$360 million-and eight deaths. Major property damage was around the epicentral area and in communities east of Los Angeles, especially the older sections of downtown Whittier, Alhambra and Pasadena where there were high concentrations of unreinforced masonry buildings that were not properly anchored to their foundations. More than 120 single-family houses and 1,300 apartments units were destroyed, and there was $20 million in damage on the Cal State University, Los Angeles, campus about six miles west of the epicenter. Tall buildings in downtown Los Angeles swayed, windows burst outward and plaster damage was widespread.

The main shock was followed by about 500 aftershocks, an unusually small number. The largest occurred on October 4 (M5.2); felt over a large area and caused another death and significant additional property damage.

This quake ended an unusual quiet period in southern California. There had not been an M4 or larger event during the previous 11 months; normally, there is an M4 quake about once a month somewhere in the southern part of the state.

November 24, 1987
SUPERSTITION HILLS
Magnitude: 6.6 Maximum MMI: VII

This was the centerpiece of an interesting series of shocks known as *The Superstition Hills sequence* on the west side of the Imperial Valley, in the lightly populated area west of Westmoreland near the Salton Sea. The sequence included two separate main shocks that originated on different faults, plus a complex aftershock pattern that included an M5.4, an M5.5, and another 30 of at least M3.5.

Because of the remote location, there were only 94 injuries and less than $5 million in damage in the valley, almost all to highways and irrigation systems. Additional injuries and damage were reported in the Mexicali area of Mexico.

Spectacular 1989 quake damage in San Francisco's Marina District resulted from a combination of insufficient structural strength and soft soils. Strong horizontal shaking was too much for buildings with open first floors or weak connections. Liquifaction of ground beneath caused differential settling. Photos by John Nakata, U. S. Geological Survey.

Interstate 880 between 16th and 34th streets in Oakland started to break up after only a few seconds of shaking, and completely pancaked after 10 to 15 seconds. Rescue efforts lasted almost two weeks. There were 42 deaths. The toll would have been higher, but traffic was unusually light, probably because of the World Series baseball game that was about to start. Photo courtesy of University of California EERC Library.

The sequence started with an M6.2 quake at 5:54 p.m. on November 23. The hypocenter was near State Highway 86 on a northeast-trending fault zone stretching from the Superstition Hills under the edge of the Salton Sea toward Niland, at a depth of little more than three miles. It was followed by a series of strong aftershocks along the same fault zone.

The next morning, November 24, there was an M6.6 quake at 5:16 a.m. This one originated on the northwest-trending Superstition Hills fault, part of the San Jacinto fault zone, with the hypocenter only 1.5 miles deep. This was followed by its own set of aftershocks.

Even though the two events are closely related, they occurred on separate, perpendicular sets of faults and are viewed as two main shocks rather than as a foreshock-main-shock or main-shock-aftershock. Epicenters were about six miles apart. Duration of strong shaking—more than 15 seconds—was unusually long for quakes of this magnitude. Both shallow quakes broke the surface. Many left-lateral ruptures were found on the northeasterly trending fault traces east of State Highway 86, with a total displacement of about five inches over an area about 10 feet wide. Ruptures on the Superstition Hills fault were predominantly right-lateral, with a maximum about six inches horizontal and less than five inches vertical. Post-earthquake creep along the Superstition Hills fault was noteworthy; by December 7, accumulated total movement had reached an maximum of 25 inches, and the creep continued for almost a year. Similar triggered creep was

recorded on earlier quakes in the Superstition Hills.

The November 24 quake was the strongest in California since 1983 (Coalinga), and was felt from San Diego to Tempe, Arizona, and throughout northern Mexico.

Though the quake sequence did not destroy any irrigation canals, there was serious buckling and breakage of canal walls. Several thousand feet of the All-American Canal that carries water from the Colorado River to the Imperial Valley slumped significantly, and State Highways 86 and 98 were closed for a short time.

This was part of a series of events in the Imperial Valley that included quakes of M6.0 or higher in 1915, 1940 (see page 99) and 1979. It is believed that the forces that caused these quakes are related to those that have pulled Baja California away from Mexico to form the Gulf of California (see page 32).

October 17, 1989
LOMA PRIETA
Magnitude 6.9 Maximum MMI: X

The largest earthquake in the San Francisco Bay Area since 1906 occurred at 5:04 p.m. (PDT), at the height of the commute hour in the San Francisco Bay Area. Sports fans throughout the country were preparing for Game 3 of the Bay Bridge World Series between the San Francisco Giants and the Oakland As.

Older sections of Oakland sustained heavy structural damage, even though the epicenter was 60 miles away. Mark Gibson photo.

In the epicentral area, cities of Santa Cruz, Watsonville, Los Gatos and Hollister all sustained major damage. In some cases, years were required to rebuild and restore local economies. Mark Gibson photo.

The hypocenter was at a depth of more than 10 miles, unusually deep for a California earthquake. The epicenter was in the Forest of Nicene Marks State Park in the Santa Cruz Mountains, nine miles northeast of the city of Santa Cruz and 60 miles southeast of San Francisco. The subsurface fault plane broke along a 30-mile section from Los Gatos to San Juan Bautista. Most people in the vicinity of the epicenter felt about 10 to 15 seconds of strong ground shaking.

As a result of this one event, the Pacific plate west of the fault moved 6.2 feet to the northwest and 4.3 feet upward over the North American plate. Surprisingly, there was no surface rupture. A complex series of secondary surface cracks and fractures damaged houses and roads, causing landslides in the Santa Cruz mountains and as far away as Hollister.

There is some argument about the exact location of the initial subsurface break. The rupture was oblique; it did not start on the same strand that broke in 1906, but joined the 1906 rupture plane on the way to the surface. There is no way of knowing if the 1989 strand broke in 1906.

Regardless of its exact location, the hypocenter certainly was within the San Andreas zone. It was the fourth known quake along strands of this particular segment. The others were in 1838, 1856 and 1906. This one was felt over 400,000 square miles from the Oregon border to Los Angeles. There were 62 deaths, more than 3,700 injuries and about $7 billion in property damage. More than 12,000 people were displaced from their homes for at least one night, 414 single-family homes were destroyed and more than 18,000 were damaged.

In the epicentral area, Santa Cruz was hardest-hit, with 3 deaths and $115 million in damage; of 602 businesses downtown before the quake, 206 were destroyed or forced to move. Among the buildings destroyed was the Pacific Garden shopping mall that lies on river deposits that also shook excessively and liquefied in the 1906 earthquake. A portion of State Highway 1 collapsed due to strong ground shaking and liquefaction of river deposits beneath the support structure. In Los Gatos, sidewalks and curbs were fractured and broken throughout much of the downtown area, due to compression. Watsonville and other smaller communities experienced severe property damage and extensive ground slumping and landsliding.

The greatest property damage was in San Francisco and Oakland, about 60 miles north of the epicenter. In San Francisco, ground shaking and damage were greatest in the poorly consolidated natural and manmade sediments on the margin of the Bay, including the Marina District and South of Market area. In the Marina, 35 buildings collapsed or were so badly damaged they had to be torn down. Most susceptible were multi-story buildings without sufficient ground-floor lateral supports. Some corner buildings suffered for lack of the stiffness and strength provided by structures on two sides.

Ferndale sustained the most damage in the 1992 quake. Despite quake occurring in the middle of a busy morning, there were no fatalities. Debris on sidewalk is mostly brick facings from buildings.

Houses in older residential areas sustained the most damage, especially those designed and built for aesthetic charm rather than strong bracing. Photos by Cheryle Easter, Eureka Times Standard.

The area that suffered the most extensive damage was under water until 1912 when it was filled with a sand-water slurry for the site of the 1915 Panama-Pacific Exposition. In one instance, a sand fountain spewed out burned remains from the 1906 earthquake and fire that was included as part of the Marina fill.

A 50-foot portion of upper deck of the then 53-year-old San Francisco-Oakland Bay Bridge collapsed; one woman was killed when the car she was driving fell into the gap. There was considerable damage to Interstate 280 in San Francisco, forcing its closure for more than three years. Reconstruction was much more difficult than expected because soil beneath the damaged section was found to be very unstable.

In the East Bay, a 3/4-mile piece of the double-deck Cypress Structure collapsed, trapping and killing 41 motorists. The failure was due to a combination of inadequate design and unstable ground conditions. The portion that collapsed was anchored in mud and filled land; portions of the freeway anchored on more solid ground farther south did not collapse. Hospitals, schools, the Bay Area Rapid Transit System and properly engineered buildings survived with minimum damage. San Francisco Airport was closed for about 13 hours due to control-tower damage. Runways at Oakland International Airport and Alameda Naval Air Station were damaged by liquefaction and lateral spreading.

Earthquakes of M5 shook the same region 15 months and two months before the October 17 quake. These may have been foreshocks; there were no others closer to the main shake. There were slightly fewer aftershocks than the average for a quake of this size; two were M5 or larger and about 50 were M4 or larger.

April 25, 1992
CAPE MENDOCINO
Magnitude 7.1 Maximum MMI: IX

This quake was damaging but not disastrous in terms of loss of life or property damage because it occurred in a sparsely populated, heavily forested section of the Coast Ranges. Even though there were about 350 injuries and $60 million in property damage from the shaking and fires, its greatest significance is scientific.

This was the first well-recorded, damaging North Coast earthquake to result from thrust-faulting along the Cascadia Subduction Zone (see page 26), which has not been seismically active during historic times. Most historic quakes in this area originated within the Gorda Plate, along the Mendocino fault that is the boundary between the Gorda and Pacific plates, or on the San Andreas fault.

There were three separate quakes—the M7.1 main shake at 11:06 a.m. (PDT) on April 25, and then another two in surprisingly quick succession, an M6.6 at 12:41 a.m. and an M6.7 at 4:18 a.m. (PDT) on April 26. The 40-second shaking in the first quake was so strong that people on the streets of Ferndale found it difficult to stand or

This downtown Ferndale store has a long earthquake history. In 1906 (left), bricks from parapet wall of what was then the General Mercantile building were thrown forward into the street. Again in 1992 (right), the same thing happened to the old building with a new name, the Valley Grocery. The building has since been demolished. Photo courtesy Humboldt Earthquake Education Center.

walk. Eye witnesses reported that the first aftershock was the most damaging to buildings. The main shock on shore was the result of thrust-faulting. Two later quakes were "triggered" strike-slip events on offshore faults—different types of movements on different types of faults. Some of the strongest ground accelerations ever recorded—nearly 2g—were produced by the first quake.

Petrolia, the closest town to the epicenter, had $1 million in damage. There was $10 million in damage in Ferndale, where 30 homes and 40 businesses were affected and utility services were interrupted. The main quake came during a parade, and while horses bolted and some people panicked, there were no fatalities. Landslides and extensive ground cracking and soil failures were common in the Mattole and Eel River valleys. There was major damage in Rio Dell and Scotia.

A tsunami generated by the offshore fault movements had maximum wave heights of about a foot at Crescent City. While there was no damage from this particular event, the fact that a sea wave was generated at all has created concern that these quakes may be forerunners of an much greater, tsunami-generating quake in the Pacific Northwest.

There was a significant uplift along a 15-mile stretch of coastline from Cape Mendocino south past the mouth of the Mattole River, as much as four feet in some areas. This killed complete intertidal communities of sealife. Other investigations of the layered plant remains in marshy inlets and estuaries have determined that different areas of the coast have been uplifted or dropped at least half a

dozen times in the last several-thousand years as the result of significant earthquakes.

June 28, 1992
LANDERS
Magnitude 7.3 Maximum MM Intensity: IX

The main shock of this largest California earthquake in 40 years was felt throughout southern California and most of southern Nevada and western Arizona. Tall buildings swayed as far away as Boise, Idaho, and Albuquerque, New Mexico. Water sloshed out of swimming pools in Denver, Colorado.

Two shocks occurred just seconds apart, on separate branches of a complex fault zone trending northwest-southeast between Interstate 15 and State Highway 62; the epicenter was near Landers, about 125 miles east of Los Angeles and 25 miles north of Palm Springs. In about half a minute, breaks progressed northward for about 40 miles into the Mojave Desert along at least five faults—some previously unknown—leaving a broad, complex trail of cracks and moletracks. Moletracks are the low earthen mounds created by ground compression (see page 82).

This was the longest surface rupture resulting from a California earthquake since 1906. Land mass east of the rupture moved about 15 feet to the right and about three feet upward relative to the landscape west of the fault. Displacement was predominantly horizontal with lesser vertical components (see page 29).

Because the strongest shaking occurred in uninhabited

The arid terrain makes 1992 Landers surface ruptures easy to follow and measure; sparse rainfall will allow escarpments to be recognizable for several years.

Landers rupture zone was as much as 40 miles wide, involving a number of parallel faults, some unknown before the earthquake.

regions of the Mojave desert, damage was modest—there was sparse population and limited commercial development along the fault;. Total property damage was less than $100 million. More than 400 people were injured, and there was one fatality—a 3-year-old child killed by a falling chimney.

Communities suffering the worst damage were Landers, Yucca Valley and Joshua Tree. Intense shaking toppled chimneys and masonry walls, shifted houses off their foundations, cracked concrete pads, broke water mains and caused power outages; landslides blocked mountain roads. The large displacement severed hundreds of underground water lines throughout the area, and shaking broke water pipes in buildings as far away as San Diego.

The Landers earthquake sequence began two months earlier, on April 22, with an M4.6 quake near Palm Springs and an M6.1 quake near Joshua Tree. There were 6,000 other shocks—most too small to be felt—between April 22 and June 28. There were so many aftershocks during the first hour after the main event, residents claimed the ground never stopped shaking. The primary M6.2 aftershock came three hours after the main event, and was actually a "triggered" quake centered on a separate fault in the San Bernardino Mountains near Big Bear Lake, about 25 miles west of the main shock epicenter. There was considerable damage and several fires in the mountain resort area; landslides and rockfalls temporarily blocked many local roads. It was the strongest of a pro-longed series of aftershocks that eventually totaled more than 40,000. Two strong aftershocks, one of M5.0, were recorded on June 17, 1994, two years to the month after the main shock.

January 17, 1994
NORTHRIDGE
Magnitude: 6.7 Maximum MMI: IX

The most costly earthquake in U.S. history, and the largest quake in the recorded history of the Los Angeles basin, occurred at 4:30 a.m. on a holiday, Martin Luther King Day. The hypocenter was about 12 miles deep on a previously unrecognized reverse fault, probably an extension of the Oak Ridge fault. The epicenter was about 20 miles northwest of downtown Los Angeles. Although there was no surface-fault rupture; large areas of secondary ground fissures and cracks were found in concrete and asphalt, especially in the San Fernando Valley—Northridge, Winnetka, Canoga Park—and in the Santa Clarita area. Landslides were common throughout the Santa Susana, San Gabriel and Santa Monica mountains, and on the Pacific Coast Highway in the Pacific Palisades area.

The 1994 and the 1971 San Fernando quakes were very similar in magnitude and intensities. Even though the epicenters were about 12 miles apart, the principal energy release occurred under a highly populated area in 1994, and beneath what was then a sparsely populated area in 1971.

The town of Joshua Tree was hit hard by the June 28, 1992, Landers earthquake. A foreshock on April 22 of the same year probably weakened some of the buildings prior to the main shock.

The official Northridge quake death toll was 60, with 33 resulting directly from the quake and the others from heart attacks and other related incidents. County hospitals treated more than 7,000 people, about 1,500 of whom required hospitalization. More than 20,000 people spent at least one night sleeping in a parking lot, park, or one of 23 Red Cross and Salvation Army shelters, including four tent cities.

Damage estimates of up to $20 billion dwarfed numbers from earlier earthquakes—the total for the 1989 Loma Prieta quake was only $7 billion. There was some damage to more than 10,000 homes. About 200 school buildings were seriously damaged or destroyed; 640 schools were closed for a day to a few weeks. Damage to utility lines left 82,000 homes and businesses without electricity, 50,000 without water, and 28,000 without natural gas. Because of interconnected power grids, there were significant electrical outages in many parts of southern California, and 150,000 customers in Idaho went without electricity for three hours.

It was not the magnitude alone that created havoc, it was the location in a highly developed urban area. Very strong ground motions contributed dramatically to the death and destruction. Ground motion was complex; shock waves crisscrossed the Los Angeles basin as they bounced off high hard-rock walls and back through softer material, creating high-energy crests and lower-energy troughs (see page 63). Peak accelerations of about 1g were recorded at a number of sites, and 1.8g was recorded at a single location in Tarzana.

The collapse of a three-level apartment house in Northridge caused 16 deaths. The building had a "soft" first floor without adequate horizontal support, and was evidently subjected to some of the strongest ground motions. The town of Fillmore was among the hardest-hit areas, with $250 million in damage, primarily on Central Avenue in the downtown business district where most structures were built of unreinforced masonry. A department store and parking garage at Northridge Fashion Center in Reseda collapsed. The failure of this and another relatively new four-story parking structure at California State University at Northridge came as a surprise; both apparently were right above the fault break. Santa Monica took a surprisingly hard hit, even though it was more than 10 miles and a mountain range away from the epicenter. Structural damage totaled $220 million, and more than 100 buildings were deemed no longer safe to occupy. St. John's Hospital sustained $25 million in damage and Santa Monica College had $26 million in damage. About 50 percent of the structures that were declared unsafe for entry were in an east-west-trending belt that lies over the Santa Monica fault zone.

As in previous earthquakes, structures engineered and built to modern standards fared far better than their older counterparts. Damage throughout the Los Angeles metropolitan area was still significant. It refocused attention on

The complex interchange of Golden State and Antelope Valley freeways in Newhall Pass was one of 11 highway structures destroyed by the 1994 quake. Overpasses were scheduled for retrofitting, but work had not been completed when they were damaged in 1971. Photo courtesy Cal State, Northridge.

Portions of a large house in Pacific Palisades overlooking Pacific Coast Highway were shaken down a steep cliff. F. M. Hanna photo.

building codes and construction quality in multi-story concrete and steel buildings, some of which did not perform as well as expected. More urgency was generated in the retrofitting of older freeways and bridges both in Los Angeles and throughout the state. Even the retrofitting standards were reopened to review, because some reinforced structures sustained significant damage even when they remained standing.

Most of the 600 miles of freeways in Los Angeles withstood the shaking, including massive structures such as the Interstate 10-Interstate 405 interchange. Portions of six freeways were closed because of damage to 10 elevated structures. A 200-foot-long concrete bridge on the Santa Monica Freeway collapsed onto the street below. The junction of the Golden State and Antelope freeways sustained major damage that required closure and extensive rerouting of traffic until May.

On Balboa Boulevard in Granada Hills, compressional and extensional movements buckled the street and sidewalks, and ruptured water and gas lines that service the neighborhood. As the gas mains and water pipe were shoved together, crumpled and then jerked back apart, both water and gas leaked up to the surface. An explosion ignited by a vehicle an hour after the quake resulted in a fire that destroyed five houses.

Memorial Coliseum was damaged enough to fear permanent closure; a nonstop repair schedule authorized by March had it renovated in time for the Fall 1994 football season. Anaheim Stadium, 50 miles from the epicenter, lost its scoreboard, some billboards, and about 1,000 seats.

This was the sixth in a series of quakes of M5.0 or greater to strike the northern Los Angeles basin since 1987, all related to a broad system of dip-slip faults related to the Transverse Ranges (see page 28). In this quake, the south side of the fault moved three to seven feet over the north side along a line about 12 miles long. As a result, Oat Mountain in the Santa Susana Mountains was elevated about 15 inches, Fillmore moved west by two inches, and Castaic Junction dropped 3.5 inches.

No recognizable foreshocks were registered. There were three concentrations of aftershocks in the first three weeks; the quantity was more than average (3,000 of M1.5 or higher), but the sequence died out faster than average. Seven were above M5.0, including an M5.3 on March 20. Four significant aftershocks came within one hour on Friday, the 21st, and five of M3.0 or more in a seven-hour period on the 29th, including one that completed the collapse of a large and presumably solid parking garage at Cal State University at Northridge.

Even with all this damage, recovery was remarkably rapid. Though there were individual tragedies and instances of inefficiency and snarled communication, the overall reconstruction effort illustrated what can be done with the proper political and financial priorities, with local cooperation, and with resilient individuals determined to rebuild homes and businesses—and their lives—as rapidly as possible. Among the most amazing recoveries was the reopening of the Santa Monica Freeway on April 12—only three months after it collapsed in what appeared to be total, irreparable ruin.

At Northridge Fashion Center, a department-store facade collapsed. Three parking structures sustained major damage. K. E. Sieh photo.

This Canoga Park apartment building was one of about 40 similar structures that collapsed because of insufficient lateral shear strength with open first-story design. Photo by P. W. Weigand.

Parking garage at California State University, Northridge, appeared structurally sound but could not stand up to quake motion. Precast-concrete interior walls lacked adequate reinforcement to withstand both vertical and horizontal movement. Chris Wills photo.

WHAT'S IN A NAME?

Naming earthquakes is not an exact science, and in some cases it has been haphazard and unfortunate.

In an attempt to give an earthquake an immediate label, the location of the first-known damage, or the suspected epicenter, is the first name applied. These names stick, even if significant new damage is uncovered in the next hours or days, or the source of the quake is reassigned.

Unfortunately, cities whose names are attached to major disasters can suffer economic consequences, from decreases in property values to diminished tourist traffic.

If property damage in a single city was the criterion, the 1906 earthquake might have been named after Santa Rosa or San Jose. If maximum surface rupture was the key, it might have gone down in history as the Pt. Reyes earthquake. However, San Francisco was the only internationally known city along the rupture zone in the early 1900s, and it was the scene of the disastrous and well-publicized fire. There was no hesitation about naming the quake.

The January 17, 1994, shock will forever be known as the *Northridge earthquake,* even though it could have been called the *San Fernando earthquake* if the name wasn't already taken. The epicenter may have been in Reseda, and Fillmore was among the hardest-hit cities. But the name that came out first was the name that stuck.

The 1989 earthquake was named after Loma Prieta, a mountain located a short distance from the epicenter, even though Santa Cruz, Watsonville, San Francisco and Oakland all sustained major damage. This successful attempt to avoid attaching a city's name to a major disaster provides an admirable example for future labeling.

Damage to freeways in the 1971 (shown here), 1989 and 1994 earthquakes has accelerated the retrofit program throughout the state and toughened the standards. Retrofitting focuses on strengthening both joints and columns. Steel cables are used to attach elevated sections to the support columns; shock absorbers help cushion the effect of the horizontal and vertical movements; and hinges link road sections to the columns below. Steel rods have always been used to give concrete columns extra strength; now, they must be wrapped much closer together than they were before 1971. Photos courtesy Cal State, Northridge.

What Lies Ahead?

Chapter 5

Seismologists may never be able to predict the time and place of future earthquakes with any precision, but it is possible to pinpoint areas and structures most likely to sustain the worst damage. The Santa Cruz mountains were the scene of widespread landsliding and slumping in the 1906 and 1989 earthquakes (below) and will certainly experience the same thing in the next major San Francisco Bay Area quake. Chris Wills photo.

It's natural for Californians to want information about future earthquakes. Advance warning would enable us to take preventive measures in time to protect ourselves and our property. Unfortunately, earthquake prediction is very elusive. This is not for a lack of effort, but because we have a small window through which to study an extremely large and complex subject.

California's recorded history is distressingly short. Reliable, detailed earthquake data of any value date back less than 150 years, scarcely a millisecond in California's geologic time clock. The forces behind the earthquakes we feel today have been building for hundreds or thousands of years.

It is a difficult, if even possible, task to apply short-term analysis to very long-term processes. We just haven't been around long enough. Unfortunately, the way to learn more about major earthquakes is to live through them. Experience is the only teacher.

One thing is known for sure: Earthquakes cannot be prevented. California will continue to have them in the future at the same approximate rate experienced since the state was settled. Stress continues to build up in the earth's crust, and the movements along faults that relieve this stress will continue unabated. Our focus has to be on mitigating the loss of life and property damage from the inevitable quakes to come.

In looking to the future, there are two separate subjects to consider:

1. Forecasting the probable locations, times and sizes of future earthquakes.

2. Predicting and mitigating the destructive effects of the earthquakes, such as loss of life, structural damage, economic disruption and civic disorder.

Future Earthquakes

The ability to forecast the probability of a quake of a certain size within a general time frame might be achievable. The ability to exactly predict the time and place for an earthquake of a specific magnitude is much more difficult and probably will never be achieved.

The basic problem is the incredible variety of earthquakes in size, location and frequency. They do not occur like clockwork—or anything close to it. Earthquakes of the 1970s and 1980s led to the chilling conclusion that any of California's faults—large or small, young or old, strike-slip or dip-slip—has the potential to move at any time and create a significant earthquake. Estimating the time of future quakes is equally frustrating. It is easy to come up with average intervals between M6.0 - 8.0 quakes on any given fault or fault segment. However, significant variations between individual events render these averages almost meaningless in terms of prediction. Only when we apply statistical percentages to long-term time frames—10 to 30 years—can any credible forecasts be made.

Complicating the problem even further is the lack of reliable, predictable precursors to earthquakes. Several elements, by themselves or in combination, could contribute to the start of a quake:

1. Long periods of accumulated stress on neighboring faults.

2. Slow creep.

3. A shift in atmospheric weather patterns.

WHAT ARE FORECASTS?

The best comparison to earthquake forecasting is weather forecasting. We routinely accept weather forecasts (not exact predictions) such as "a 70% chance of rain in the Los Angeles basin over the next weekend." Attempts to predict the exact time the rain will begin, the exact area that will get wet, and the exact amount that will fall are difficult at best, with a very low accuracy rate.

We must also accept forecasts of "a 70% chance of an M7.5 earthquake on the Coachella Valley segment of the San Andreas fault in the next 25 years," without a specific prediction of exact time, location and size.

In either case, there is a 30% chance the forecasted event will not happen. We still should carry our raincoats and umbrellas when we go out over the weekend because it probably will rain in the forecasted time frame. We should also set up and implement similar protective "umbrellas" to minimize damage if the earthquake happens in the forecasted time frame.

Weather and earthquake forecasts differ in one significant aspect. With weather, there are both long-term weather records and short-term, observable phenomena that always precede storms—the change of seasons, temperature variations, advancing weather fronts, wind patterns, etc.

With earthquakes, we have only historical, statistical data. "Short-term" as we understand it does not apply in geology, and there are no consistent, observable precursors to fault movements.

Southern California basins have the double danger of many faults packed close together, plus dense population centers with commercial centers and transportation networks. This combination makes it difficult to forecast which fault or fault segment is most likely to break next, and to minimize quake damage that results.

4. The tides.
5. A change in the elevation or tilt of a rock formation.
6. Changes in electromagnetic fields.
7. Dramatic alterations in water content of rocks.

This last element, *fluid content*, is the current prime suspect, but as of late 1994, no precursor could be labeled as the key.

Recent earthquakes have not been any help. Rather than reaffirming scientific theories, they have only added to the confusion. New data have refuted some basic concepts about the nature of earthquakes—it turns out they are much more complicated than originally thought. Even the most basic concepts are open to question. Knowledge of the state's geology and seismology is inadequate, and may never be adequate because of their complexity.

Despite these problems, geologists and seismologists continue to make best efforts at forecasting, with some interesting results.

Where Will Future Earthquakes Occur?

This is the easiest question to answer generally, but not specifically. Future California earthquakes will occur on one of the state's faults (see page 23.) Unfortunately, it has become apparent in the last 30 years that there are many more faults with the potential to create earthquakes that we thought existed in the 1960s. The largest, with conspicuous surface features, are well mapped. Countless others buried beneath the surface are difficult to locate, much less map over their entire length.

Despite the difficulties, the geologic-mapping process continues, using sophisticated technology. Modern instrumentation introduced since the 1970s has enabled geologists to map faults in much greater detail. Sensitive instruments deployed in tight networks reveal the slightest tremors and identify their sources. Dipping fault planes can be identified more readily, and aftershock patterns can be analyzed to delineate the fracture zones.

In the early 1990s, a major attempt was made to identify subsurface formations by setting off a series of below-surface explosions both offshore of Southern California and inland as far east as Barstow. Underwater blasts were created with compressed air, and underground with explosives. Seismograms recorded the travel paths and speeds of the resulting sound waves, and analysis may reveal the location of previously unrecognized faults. A similar project mapped the bottom of San Francisco Bay in 1992 and 1993.

Even with detailed mapping, the big problem is trying to figure out which fault will break next. A fault map of California is a scary thing. Fractures split the state in every direction, especially in Southern California. A map of earthquake epicenters is equally impressive. Again, Southern California shows the most variation—one geologist suggests that the area map "looks like a shotgun has been fired at it."

When faults are lined up close together, as they are in and around the Los Angeles basin, it is impossible to determine those that are accumulating the most strain and are therefore most likely to break.

Even though it's not possible to pinpoint the location of future quakes, scientists are doing everything possible to generate probability scenarios for different parts of the state. These statistically supportable probability scenarios greatly influence zoning regulations, building codes,

The 1994 Northridge quake not only caused damage over a wide area (Rosemead shown above), it significantly altered the stress on faults throughout southern California. Photo Los Angeles County Fire Department.

RECENT STRESS CHANGES

Analysis of quakes during the last three decades indicates that each event affects a much wider area than previously thought. Here are examples of stress changes resulting from recent earthquakes, based on geophysical models:

1. The 1989 Loma Prieta quake increased the stress load on the San Andreas fault on the northern San Francisco peninsula. It decreased the load on the Hayward and Calaveras faults in the East Bay—at least temporarily. This caused scientists to change the probability status on both for the two years following Loma Prieta. After that time, yet another forecast was required because the normal tectonic-stress accumulation had made up for any temporary relaxation caused in 1989.

2. The 1992 Landers/Big Bear earthquakes caused changes in regional stress that pushed much of the southern San Andreas fault closer to failure. Higher than normal levels of earthquake activity were recorded in the months after June 28. The probability forecast for a major event on the southernmost segment of the San Andreas fault system was increased.

3. The 1994 Northridge quake increased load on part of the San Gabriel fault. Stress on the section of the San Andreas near Palmdale was increased the equivalent of 1-3 years of normal tectonic loading.

Similar adjustments were caused by all of the significant quakes in the state, including those in Kern County in 1952 (see page 100) and Imperial Valley in 1940 (see page 99).

It could well be that the quake expected in Parkfield between 1987-1993 (see page 47) was delayed because stress in the rocks was relieved by other fault movements, most notably the thrust faulting only 20 miles away that caused the 1983 Coalinga earthquake.

emergency-center preparations, and preparedness by utility companies. The probabilities change often, because earthquakes affect each other. One fault movement may increase or decrease the stress of adjacent parts of the same fault, and on other faults in the same general region, thereby increasing or decreasing the probabilities.

When Will They Occur?

Public agencies that respond to public inquiries report that the most asked question is: "When is the next Big One going to happen?" Unfortunately, forecasting even approximate dates of future events is a difficult challenge. Historical data often create more questions than answers.

One theory postulates that faults break in segments; the San Andreas, and other major faults, will never break over their entire length all at once. Segments are defined by changes in physical expression (range fronts, changes in orientation of scarps); fault geometry (bends, lateral steps to meet other faults within the same zone); seismicity (limits of previous surface ruptures, different slip rates, areas of creep); or intersecting structures (branching or intersecting faults, cross ridges, bodies of water).

Segments range in length from a few to dozens of miles; there are about 20 segments on the San Andreas fault. Each displays different behavior; some are active, others not. Those segments with a geologic record of activity within the last 11,000 years, but distinctly fewer recent earthquakes compared to other segments, are called *seismic* gaps. The most significant seismic gap on the San Andreas Fault (actually a continuous string of smaller segments) is between the southern end of the 1906 rupture near San Juan Bautista and the northern end of the 1857 rupture near Parkfield.

In these gaps where the fault has been stuck together for longer periods without any movement, the strain accumulation is greater, and quakes should be more likely to occur. Using the long-term slip rate, and the amount of slip generated by each earthquake, the recurrence interval (average time between earthquakes) on that particular segment or fault can be estimated.

However, this theory is difficult to reconcile with California's historical seismicity. Most faults and fault segments are not well behaved, and will not conform to the desired predictable patterns. Big earthquakes sometimes break several segments, and often reoccur over and over on the same segments rather than in seismic gaps.

Average recurrence cycles vary widely. By using a frequency-magnitude relation log, it can be estimated that along the San Andreas fault, there is an even chance of one M6.0 event within any 15-month interval, one M7.0 event within a 12.5-year interval, or one of M8.0 within any 125-year period. However, reality differs markedly from the mathematical projection. Averages on different sites range anywhere from 125-400 years, with actual intervals much more variable.

In the Carrizo Plain, measurements of offsets and subsequent determination of the slip rate indicate that the interval between large quakes may be as much as 300 years. Farther south, the San Jacinto fault has been much more active, having produced at least nine M6.0 or greater

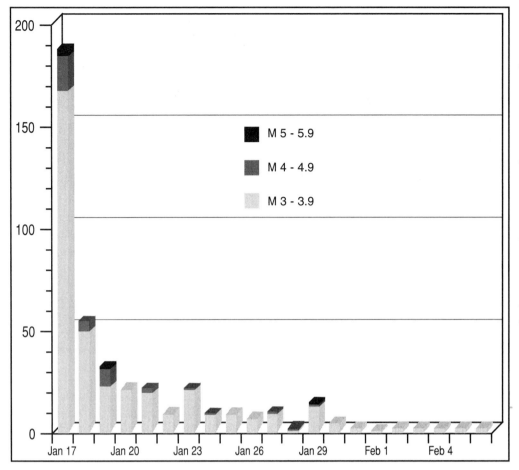

	M 5 - 5.9
	M 4 - 4.9
	M 3 - 3.9

One of the few predictable aspects of a major earthquake is the aftershock pattern. The number and size of aftershocks will seldom vary significantly from computer models seismologists have created, based on data from past quakes. Diagram shows number of aftershocks of M3 or greater recorded per day during four weeks following the January 17,1994 Northridge earthquake. Number of M3-3.9 aftershocks is shown in light gray. M4-4.9 in medium gray, and M5-5.9 in black. Chart courtesy California Division of Mines and Geology.

quakes since 1890. The average recurrence interval is about 10 years, with the longest interval 19 years.

Carbon dating of peat deposits at Pallett Creek near Palmdale has established the dates of earthquakes on the San Andreas fault in that area as:

500 A.D.	1100
671	1346
734	1480
797	1812
997	1857
1048	

The margin of error for each quake is estimated at less than 50 years. The average interval is 125, with the greatest time lapse as 332 years (1480-1812) and the shortest 45 (1812-1857). The most common interval is 50-75 years.

These very erratic patterns clearly show the problems involved in trying to use historical averages to predict future events except in very broad time scales. It also challenges the idea that fault segments always break when they reach some consistent, predictable point of critical stress (see below).

These variables defeat prediction attempts, and drive scientists to fits of despair. Even where activity on a short fault segment is thought to be predictable, such as Parkfield (see page 47), the probable result is disappointment. Still, scientists continue to make best efforts in selecting those faults that pose the greatest threats.

How Big Will They Be?

The size of earthquakes since 1800 has been fairly well documented, and enough surface and below-ground evidence is available to allow geologists to make some educated guesses about activity over the last 2,000 years. With this data in hand, scientists have tried to define a "characteristic earthquake" for each fault or fault segment.

Theoretically, scientists can estimate an average earthquake for faults or fault segments where there are records of at least two quakes. The more events in the historical record, the more accurate the estimate. It is assumed that the slip rate is constant, and the amount of stress buildup required to break the fault is constant over the long term. The resistance of the rocks shouldn't change, so there should be movement every time the stress level reaches the same break point.

On the San Andreas fault, there have been only two major quakes during historic times—1857 and 1906. Even though they broke on different "locked" segments, they were very similar in magnitude and length of surface rupture. When the next big quake comes on either of those segments, it is assumed that it will be of characteristic magnitude, M7.5-8.0. The surface rupture will be about the same length.

However, many geologists refute this theory. They point out that the variability in the intervals between quakes at Pallett Creek indicated the stress required to break a fault segment is not constant, and is subject to a

"THE BIG ONE"

If there is a repeat of the 1857 or 1906 quakes, it will be a much different disaster than those created by the 1989 Loma Prieta and 1994 Northridge earthquakes. Energy release will be far greater than anything felt in California since 1906. Shaking will last from one to three minutes. Intensities will vary considerably, but the duration alone will be a major cause of damage. Even the best-designed and best-built structures close to the epicenter will be susceptible to major damage.

If the surface rupture approximates those of the 1857 and 1906 quakes, all highways, utility trunk lines, and water aqueducts that cross the fault will be offset by as much as 15-20 feet, with a disastrous interruption of daily services. More low-frequency, long-period waves will roll out over long distances and cause different types of building damage, particularly in high-rises that are most susceptible to the long wave lengths.

Estimates of death and total destruction vary, depending on the location of the epicenter. A repeat of the 1906 quake poses the greater threat, because of the heavy commercial and residential development close to the fault between Humboldt County and San Juan Bautista, the area most affected in 1906. A repeat of the 1857 quake means a surface rupture from Cholame to Wrightwood, an area where development is sparse—at least close to the fault. However, downtown Los Angeles is less than 75 miles from Fort Tejon, location of the 1857 epicenter.

A repeat of the 1906 earthquake would produce shock waves lasting far longer than that of any recent quake, and will cause significant damage from Crescent City to Hollister. In 1906, all cities on the bay side of the San Francisco Peninsula sustained major damage, including San Jose where the Hotel Vendome completely collapsed.

wide variety of unpredictable circumstances. Forecasts of "characteristic earthquakes" made in the 1970s and 1980s have not turned out to be accurate. Even the quake given highest probability—at Parkfield—did not occur in the projected 1987-1993 time frame.

Characteristic or not, a damaging earthquake has occurred in and around the Los Angeles basin at an average of every 15-20 years for at least two centuries. And there's no reason to believe this pattern will change. Activity in this area was less than expected between 1800 and 1985, but the rate of M5.0 and greater events has doubled since 1986. This pattern may continue if the latest stress estimates are correct. Quakes in the M6.0-7.0 class pose a much more consistent threat to Southern Californians than the "Big One"—the M7.5-8.0 on the San Andreas fault.

This is not to belittle the importance of the San Andreas fault—it remains the longest in the state, with the fastest slip rate, and the greatest potential for M7.5-8.0 quakes. Thus it will always pose the greatest risk to Californians.

Destructive Effects of Earthquakes

Even if it is impossible to predict the exact time, place and size of fault movements, it is possible to predict the destructive effects of earthquakes, whenever they arrive.

Damage prediction is well on the way to becoming a well-defined science. Each quake brings some surprises—but fewer and fewer. We now know enough about effects

to be able to delineate and weigh the hazards, and take necessary steps to minimize death and destruction. Major earthquakes are going to cause major disruptions in public and private life; however, the degree can be reduced significantly by public and personal action. It is often said that *ignorance* is the most costly factor in earthquake damage. A great deal of data is available on hazards, and if we learn from history, losses can be greatly reduced.

It is very expensive and time-consuming—perhaps even impossible within realistic cost constraints—to design and build everything to withstand an M8+ quake. It is possible to set building codes and emergency procedures to minimize the damage from the M6.0-M7.0 quakes that have caused all the death and destruction since 1906.

Local areas with hazardous geologic features can be mapped in great detail, and the severity and duration of shaking for earthquakes of every size can be predicted for different types of soil. These potential problems can be identified:

1. Localities where the ground is most likely to fail because of surface ruptures, liquefaction or landsliding.

2. Existing structures most likely to collapse because of inadequate design and construction standards.

3. Weak links in transportation and utility networks, usually those that either cross active faults or are in areas subject to landslides and secondary ground slumping.

SAN FRANCISCO'S PRECARIOUS POSITION

San Francisco usually is pictured east of the San Andreas fault; in fact it is caught up in a series of fault branches that resemble the tines of a pitchfork. These are the main faults, from west to east:

1. The San Gregorio-Hosgri fault diverges from the main trace of the San Andreas at Bolinas Bay. It lies just offshore of San Mateo County, comes ashore briefly at San Gregorio, and then goes underwater again at Point Ano Nuevo south of Monterey Bay.
2. The Pilarcitos fault, currently dormant, is traceable from Pedro Point, about five miles south of Mussel Rock, along the north side of Montara Mountain as far south as Los Altos Hills.
3. The current line of most recent activity in the San Andreas zone lies under the ocean west of San Francisco, comes on land at Mussel Rock and passes under San Andreas Lake and Crystal Springs Reservoirs.
4. The Hayward fault runs along on the east side of the Bay. The Rodgers Creek fault north of San Pablo Bay carries its own name, but is linked to the Hayward fault via a short step.
5. The Calaveras fault zone includes the Green Valley and Concord faults to the north and south of Suisun Bay, and a southern section in Contra Costa and Alameda counties.

If the faults east of the bay turn out to be as active as suspected, the city of San Francisco could find itself in a precarious position, caught between the San Gregorio, Pilarcitos, and San Andreas on one side, and the Hayward/Calaveras zones on the other.

The San Francisco Bay Area faults already have generated a long string of significant quakes between San Pablo Bay and Hollister—1836 (M6.7), 1838 (M7.0), 1865 (M6.3), 1868 (M7.0), 1892 (M6.4), 1897 (M6.5), 1898 (M6.5), 1906 (M7.7), 1911 (M6.6) and 1989 (M6.9)—more than any other similar-sized area of California in the state's short historical record. It is significant that only two on this list occurred after 1906 (see page 8).

The San Andreas fault has been responsible for some of the state's biggest quakes, including 1906 (above), but in the last half of the 20th century, lesser-known—often unrecognized—faults have caused the most trouble. Courtesy of California Division of Mines and Geology.

There aren't many mysteries here. If the San Jacinto fault ruptures in the San Bernardino area, the freeway interchange of Interstates 10 and 215 will sustain major damage because it sits right on top of the fault. Cajon Pass will be the site of major damage—to the highway, communication links, power and utility lines—and it may be closed for several days. There will be major landslides both in the pass and in the mountains around Mt. Baldy.

The cornerstones to minimizing loss of life and property damage in this or any other major California quake are:

1. Regional planning based on geologic knowledge.
2. Strictly enforced building codes for new construction.
3. Strengthening existing structures.
4. Effective emergency preparedness.

All of these have improved since the 1960s, so the state was much better prepared for the 1994 Northridge quake than for the 1971 San Fernando quake, and it will be even better prepared for the next one.

Scientists and public safety officials continue to improve their communication of pertinent data, and their interaction in times of emergency. State and local agencies know what to do and many businesses are prepared to avoid or minimize disruptions in transportation, power, and communications. A growing number of individuals is assuming responsibility for preparing themselves and their homes. Despite heavy tolls in the 1989 Loma Prieta and 1994 Northridge quakes, all the numbers would have been worse without these efforts.

Retrofitting hazardous structures reduces the risk, but not to the same degree as building safe structures in the first place. Even though there were some surprising failures in multi-story concrete-and-steel buildings in the 1994 Northridge earthquake, overwhelming evidence proved proper seismic design pays off. Structures designed and built to the most recent seismic design provisions of the California Uniform Building Codes with stood the forces very well. Those built to lesser code provisions suffered much more extensive damage.

It is important to keep in mind that risk is not uniform in any one county, town or even neighborhood. What happens to an individual structure depends on interrelationship of:

1. Distance from the epicenter.
2. Local soil conditions.
3. Age of structure and type of construction.
4. Nature of the shock waves.

Damage usually decreases rapidly with distance from the earthquake source, but soft ground and poorly designed buildings can make distant areas much more subject to damage than modern buildings on solid ground very close to the quake (see page 74).

Recurrence frequency is on our side. Fortunately, big quakes are separated by many years—valuable time that can be used to increase geological and seismological knowledge, to strengthen buildings and freeways, to tear down old dangerous offices and homes and replace them with those of modern design and construction, and to continue to improve emergency procedures.

LEGISLATIVE AFTERSHOCKS

Earthquake aftershocks are not confined to fault zones; they extend into the California legislature as well. After each major quake in the state, there is renewed interest in passing legislation to create and fund programs intended to mitigate loss of life and property damage in the next big quake.

The 1906 earthquake was the first to focus attention on California quakes, and the need to set up a State Earthquake Investigation Commission. The 1925 Santa Barbara, 1933 Long Beach, and 1940 earthquakes led to the enactment of new design and construction standards for public buildings. The most important legislation following the 1933 quake was the Field Act that established earthquake-resistant standards for all new public-school construction.

More recent quakes have led to the development of programs intended to limit new construction in areas of highest earthquake danger. The 1971 San Fernando quake gave rise to the 1972 Alquist-Priolo Earthquake Fault Zoning Act and the 1972 Hospital Safety Act. It also includes the requirement that a Seismic Safety Element be included in the general plan of each city and county in California. The Seismic Safety Commission was created in 1974.

The Alquist-Priolo Earthquake Fault Zoning Act

This legislation represents the state's first effort at a mandatory zoning law to mitigate geologic hazards. Intended to eliminate death, injury and building damage due to fault ruptures, it requires the California Division of Mines and Geology to map all known active faults in California and to designate areas within about 500 feet of these faults as Special Earthquake Fault Zones.

Before any new housing subdivision can be approved in these zones, the developer must call in a consulting geologist to establish the exact location of the fault, and to determine whether it is active or dormant. Buildings intended for human occupancy must be set back from faults judged to be active, with the actual amount (usually 50 feet) determined by local governments. The area over the fault can be covered with streets, parking lots, green belts or similar buffers.

An active fault is one that is well-defined at or just below the surface and has been active within the last 11,000 years. By 1994, more than 100 faults were mapped. The process continues as new evidence is uncovered on existing or previously unknown faults capable of surface ruptures.

The usual methods of defining a fault and determining its recent activity include interpretations of aerial photos, field mapping and paleoseismologic studies (see page 27). One or more trenches are dug 5-15 feet deep across the fault, through soil and alluvium, down to the top layers of rock. Geologists then examine and map the layers of soil, looking for offsets, bits of carbon that can be dated, and other evidence that there has been movement along the fault within the last 11,000 years.

Faults that do not break the surface (including hidden thrust faults) or have a wide and diffuse rupture pattern are difficult to define and are not zoned. Only those faults that break the surface as reasonably well-defined ruptures can be effectively avoided.

The Seismic Hazards Mapping Act

This legislation was enacted in 1990, after the 1989 Loma Prieta quake. It requires the Division of Mines and Geology to map earthquake-prone metropolitan areas of California to reveal sites most likely to sustain major damage from ground motion, liquefaction and landslides—additional seismic hazards not covered by the Alquist-Priolo Act.

These maps are compiled by computer analysis of geologic, soil and engineering data, plus aerial photos. Electronic photomapping techniques match subsurface geologic formations with surface developments.

The result is a series of digital maps that are made available to local governments, land developers, residents and other interested parties to help them determine if an existing building or future project is within a danger zone. Developers are required to hire consultants to evaluate sites and provide plans to deal with the hazards before local governments can approve construction.

As with the Alquist-Priolo Act, potential seismic hazards must be reported in sellers' disclosures to buyers of existing properties in Seismic Hazards Zones.

Financial support of the program has been haphazard. Because funding is tied to new construction, resources dwindled during California's economic recession of the early 1990s. To make matters worse, another major source of funds disappeared when the short-lived California Residential Earthquake Recovery Act was repealed in the 1992 state legislative session. The situation improved after the 1994 Northridge quake, when the federal Emergency Management Agency provided accelerated funding for immediate seismic zoning of the region impacted by the quake. This funding permitted seismic zoning of high-risk portions of Los Angeles, Orange and Ventura counties to be completed in just a few years. Seismic hazards in all of California's principal urban areas will be charted by the year 2000, and in major growth areas before 2010.

Modern design and construction standards will not prevent superficial cracking and minor structural damage (left). But single-family residences are much more likely to maintain their structural integrity while those built much earlier, especially before 1933 (right), are likely to collapse because of inadequate reinforcement.

A required setback from Hayward Fault in Fremont resulted in greenbelt between new houses. Chris Wills photo.

Trenches cut through active faults reveal evidence of movement within the last 11,000 years. Earl Hart photo.

Since the 1906 earthquake (above), there have been only two major quakes on the northern section of the San Andreas fault. Some seismologists believe this area will generate a big shake within the next few decades.

Horizontal bracing can minimize this type of damage to residential homes. One-story wood-frame dwellings generally perform well in moderate earthquakes, but only if they can withstand sharp lateral movements caused by shock waves.

FAULTS WITH HIGHEST EARTHQUAKE POTENTIAL

Several faults and fault segments are identified as probable sites for quakes before the year 2020, including Parkfield, the Mojave segment of the San Andreas fault, and the San Jacinto fault. Two regions appear to have the highest potential:

1. The San Francisco Bay Area. On this broad section of the San Andreas fault system, there is ample evidence that we are entering the phase of increased regional activity after a long aseismic period. There were seven damaging earthquakes of M6.5 or greater in the San Francisco Bay region during the 83 years prior to 1906. Only two damaging earthquakes occurred in the 83 years after 1906,

including Loma Prieta in 1989. This paucity of activity indicates that the 1906 quake did a good job of relieving strain throughout the region.

However, measurements indicate stress has been accumulating at a normal rate since 1906, with only partial relief provided by the two quakes. Could some of the fault segments that broke in 1906 be very close to reaching a failure level again?

2. The southernmost part of the state, between San Gorgonio Pass and the Mexican border, especially the Coachella Valley segment of the San Andreas fault. Not a single large earthquake has occurred in historic times on the Banning and Indio sections of the San Andreas system south of San Bernardino.

Field research indicates that the last one was about 1680, and the repeat interval in this area is about 230 years. Recent activity shares many similarities with the situation in the San Francisco Bay region before 1906—an absence of quakes on the San Andreas fault itself, and a high level of activity in the other faults around it.

The basic California seismic cycle starts with a major earthquake, then a low level of seismicity as the after-shocks subside, a rise in regional activity as strain accumulates, and ulti-mately the occurrence of another earthquake that initiates the next cycle. Both the San Francisco Bay Area and the Coachella Valley appear to be in third phase of the cycle.

Parkfield is the scene of the most intense data-collecting effort in the state. Lasers are only one of the tools used to monitor minute shifts in the earth's crust. John K. Nakata photo.

EARTHQUAKE-MONITORING DEVICES

Data on stress buildup and release along faults is gathered not only with laboratory seismographs, but also with a variety of sophisticated monitoring devices installed in the field. Where these devices are located varies, depending on the forecasts of earthquakes and slow creep on particular fault segments. Measurements taken by these devices may prove critical in forecasting future quakes. An apparently significant new reading from a single device is usually viewed with skepticism. Confirmation, or "correspondence between instruments," is necessary to validate changes.

Magnitudes are measured on three-component seismometers, the most sensitive of which are installed in boreholes to pick up the slightest tremors beneath the surface. These, plus strong motion instruments at ground level, can be used to study seismic waves from the smallest foreshocks to major ruptures.

Movements of land masses on opposite sides of faults are measured by observing changes in the horizontal and vertical positions of fixed benchmarks via triangulation networks. Two-color laser geodimeters provide precise measurements and can detect even minute horizontal deformations. Global Positioning System (GPS) receivers that pick up radio signals from 24 orbiting satellites add another dimension. These space-age devices were developed first by the U.S. Defense Department as military and commercial navigational tools. They also are valuable to geologists in making precise measurements of latitude, longitude and elevation of benchmarks within less than an inch. New measurements are taken periodically during aseismic periods, and always after earthquakes. Also, GPS measurements are being used to measure the compression rate across the Los Angeles basin, which appears to be about a quarter inch per year.

Stress changes in the rocks on either side of the fault are measured with strainmeters, delicate instruments lowered into deep boreholes. They can precisely measure deformations of less than one part per million.

Water levels in wells are monitored with pressure transducers, floats or even acoustic systems that detect changes caused by increases or decreases of stress in the rocks that either squeeze or stretch underground water reservoirs.

Changes in the earth's magnetic fields are measured by magnetometers. Data can be difficult to gather where man-made activities create interference, but magnetometers are effective in all but the busiest urban areas.

Changes in electrical fields related to moisture content and conductivity are measured by placing electrodes in the ground a few miles apart and measuring the potential resistance between them.

Rotation or "tilt" in the rock formations at the surface that may indicate a pending movement along the fault is detected and measured by tiltmeters.

The usually steady, sometimes erratic creep that characterizes certain fault segments is measured by creepmeters, surface devices with wires or rods stretched across the fault. They constantly monitor both amount and rate of the movement.

Immediately after a major earthquake, portable measuring devices are rushed into the field. Within a week after the 1994 Northridge earthquake, 75 portable instruments were operating to measure new changes in stress and the aftershock patterns on both the source fault and all others in the same general area.

Earthquake Preparedness

Chapter 6

This map, widely distributed in the San Francisco Bay Area, is one of many publications available to help residents of Earthquake Country assess possible damage to their homes in future earthquakes. Map courtesy of Geomatrix Consultants and U.S. Geological Survey.

Potential for serious earthquake damage in California is increasing. As the state continues to develop, a greater portion of the population encroaches upon active seismic zones in coastal areas. When the 1906 earthquake struck, it affected a population of about 500,000. It was a catastrophe in terms of fatalities and property damage. What can we expect if a similar earthquake occurs now that the population of the same area approaches 6,000,000 people?

Because disastrous earthquakes are infrequent events, it is very easy to postpone preventive measures, especially when they involve extra expenses and work. After all, the next big quake might not come for another 10 years, or even in your lifetime. But it might occur today or tomorrow.

The earthquakes of the 1970s and 1980s have taught us that preparedness works. Homes and workplaces can be modified to minimize property damage. People can make some simple lifestyle adjustments that can have major beneficial effects when the shaking starts.

Detailed information on every aspect of earthquake preparedness in homes, offices and schools is readily available in special publications issued by the government agencies listed on page 140. Still more information is found in general-interest books and magazines available at bookstores and newsstands. Presented here are some of the most important considerations.

Strengthening and Repairing Your Home

If you are serious about minimizing earthquake danger to your family and your home, you must evaluate the condition of the existing structure first. Target the areas in greatest need for improvement. If the necessary repairs are beyond your knowledge and talents—and they probably are—you won't have to look very far to find professional assistance.

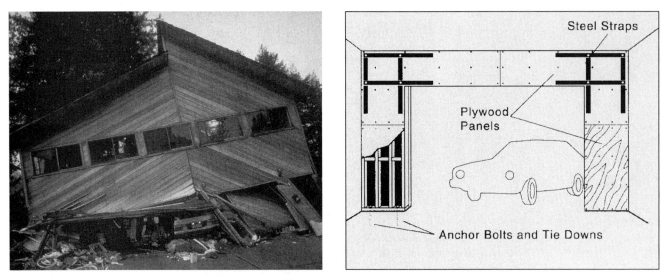

California's climate and lifestyle encourage construction of buildings that take advantage of the mild weather and attractive hillside sites. Unfortunately, these structures often cannot withstand strong, complicated earthquake waves. This Santa Cruz mountains home was built over a garage that was not strong enough to withstand the 1989 quake. Diagram illustrates how to minimize garage damage with proper wall bracing. Photo and diagram courtesy of California Seismic Safety Commission Homeowner's Guide to Earthquake Safety.

First, take the time to inform yourself about earthquake hazards and possible solutions. Even if you don't understand all the technical details, try to familiarize yourself with the concepts involved so you will be able to select the right people to do the jobs. Quality improvements can make a major difference in the damage to your home in the next quake.

Next, determine the earthquake potential for your home site; Fault-zone maps and general-soils maps are available at city and county planning offices, and through government agencies. If you find that your house is in an active fault zone, an area of unstable soil, or subject to landsliding, you may want to take some remedial steps.

Local building departments have all the details on residential codes. Civil and structural engineers and architects have available a huge data base of information about building techniques and quality controls. Geologists, foundation engineers and geotechnical engineers are trained and licensed to evaluate soil conditions and recommend appropriate action. Licensed and experienced contractors have the knowledge and personnel needed to do the actual work.

In general, horizontal bracing is the key to minimizing damage. The type of bracing varies with different types of buildings—wood frame, concrete, and steel. Earthquake forces tend to concentrate around doors and windows, so extra support is usually needed. Here are some other considerations:

1. What is the condition of the house's foundation? Some older homes were built on wood beams laid directly on the ground, or on unreinforced masonry walls. Both are very unstable during an earthquake. If you have a concrete foundation, check it for crumbling and make sure the house is anchored to it properly. This is a common repair, and the techniques are well known.

2. What is the age of your home? If it was built before 1930, some structural elements such as mortar and wood joints may be deteriorating with age, or termite and dry-rot damage may require repair. An old chimney in questionable condition can be tied to the house with metal straps. The upper structure can be replaced with metal flues. The taller the chimney above the roof line, the harder it can fall.

3. Is excess glass a problem? Tempered or laminated glass can be installed, or old windows can be covered with acrylic sheeting to strengthen the glass and hold it together if shattered.

4. What is the condition of the plumbing and wiring systems? They should operate efficiently, and lines should be strapped down to minimize damage during a quake.

5. Are porches and decks firmly attached to the house? If the connection is weak, the two structures could separate during a major quake and the porch would almost certainly collapse.

6. Are you ready for a new roof? If so, consider lightweight, fireproof materials, and make sure the sheathing is solid. Chimneys may require extra support or replacement at the same time as the new roof is installed.

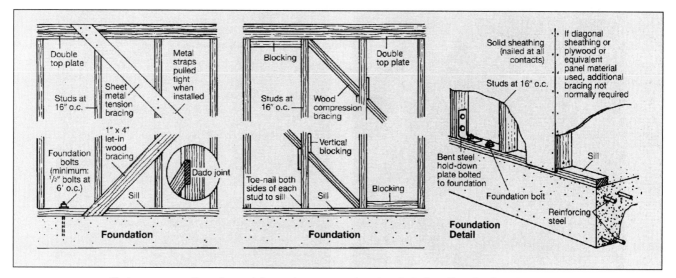

To increase earthquake resistance in new construction, bolt the sill to the foundation and nail all studs to the sill. Install cross-wall bracing in opposing pairs, either as an X or V. Sketch shows how extra resistance can be added with plywood sheathing and hold-down plates. Complete information on building earthquake-resistance into a new home or a remodel can be obtained from sources listed on page 140. Always consult a structural engineer before making major alterations to an existing structure.

7. Are there "cripple walls" between the foundation and the first floor of the house to create a crawl space? These require sturdy plywood bracing to resist the horizontal shaking that typifies earthquakes. Similar improvements may be needed on a house with a pier-and-post foundation.

8. Look everywhere on the property for walls made of unreinforced masonry: bricks, hollow clay tiles, stone, concrete blocks or adobe. They may be part of the house facing, property-line fences, mail-box supports or garden decoration. Because these walls cannot resist horizontal shaking, they collapse even in moderate quakes. It is difficult to reinforce an existing structure; an architect or engineer is the best source of advice.

Furniture and Personal Possessions

Furniture and personal belongings pose a double problem in a major earthquake. They can fall or topple over and be the cause of personal injuries, and they can break easily. The best policy is to secure everything you can to the frame of the house, and install devices necessary to keep small objects from falling. Here are some steps to take to minimize the potential damage:

1. Move heavy items such as pictures, mirror and tall dressers away from your bed. You spend a third of your time there, and the chart on page 12 indicates that almost half the magnitude M6.5 earthquakes between 1800 and 1994 occurred between 10 p.m. and 7 a.m.

2. Secure tall furniture, bookcases, filing cabinets and large workshop tools to wall studs with lag bolts or L-brackets. Most can be installed so they are invisible to residents and visitors.

3. Move heaviest objects from top to bottom shelves. Add lips to shelves to prevent items from sliding off, and secure cupboards with latches that will prevent the doors from opening during a quake.

4. Fasten heavy or precious items to shelves or tables with commercial fastening devices or adhesive compounds.

5. Whenever possible, secure computers, television sets, and stereo equipment with brackets and straps.

6. Make sure overhead light fixtures are securely fastened to the ceiling; the tubes in fluorescent fixtures can be secured with wire.

7. Store cleaners, chemicals and other potentially dangerous materials in secure containers and in sturdy cabinets, on the floor if possible.

Preventive Measures Before an Earthquake

Most importantly, have an emergency plan and share it with members of your family, co-workers, and people in the neighborhood. Here are some measures to keep in mind:

1. Post a list of emergency phone numbers in case the telephone is working. However, your emergency plan should work if telephone service is unavailable. Immediately after a major quake, thousands of people do the same thing at the same time—they pick up the phone and call home, school or a spouse at work, or an emergency center.

Interior damage can be minimized by using commercial devices to anchor cabinets to walls, prevent large drawers from opening, and keep cabinet doors from swinging open. Even lamps and computers can be anchored securely. Objects on shelves and countertops are likely to bounce off their places unless secured with museum wax or a similar adhesive. P.W. Weigand photos.

The phone system overloads very quickly. Public pay phones always remain operable in emergencies, so it's a good idea to find those closest to your home.

2. As valuable as it may be as a communications tool, don't count on your home computer to call for help or exchange information. Electric power frequently is disrupted in a major quake, and even if it is operational, lack of telephone service will render the modem useless.

3. Everyone has to know what to do in different situations. Adults in workplaces and children in school will have the most help and support. Those at home will have to make their own decisions, often without help from any official emergency agency.

4. Members of your family may be separated right after the quake; they should have in mind a safe place where everyone can reunite. Designate a single family member or friend as the central clearing point for information; everyone should contact this person as soon as possible about their whereabouts and condition. If you have children in school, ask about the policy concerning their release after an earthquake. Instruct your children on what to do and where to go if they are released before you can contact them.

5. Everyone who lives in your house should know the location of main gas, electric, and water control points, and how to shut them off. Buy the special wrench that fits your gas turnoff valve. Show family members how to use it and fasten it next to the valve.

6. Have on hand information on how to provide first aid, fight fires and help people trapped under debris. This is available from the American Red Cross or other agencies listed on page 140. The introductory pages of most telephone directories include sections on First Aid.

7. Keep emergency supplies on hand. The most useful, and fortunately the most common, are a flashlight with live batteries, a battery-operated radio that works, a decent first-aid kit, and an A-B-C-rated fire extinguisher. A roll of duct tape could be useful in making minor repairs. Plastic bags, gloves, crescent wrenches, blankets and some rope are other good items to have available. A Citizens Band (CB) radio could also be helpful. If you live in a remote location, you may decide to keep extra supplies of water and food on hand. If so, locate them in a safe place that is accessible to all members of your family. Replace the items periodically--water goes bad, cans leak, perishable goods perish. Detailed checklists for emergency tools and supplies are available from the agencies listed on page 140.

Special Considerations for the Young, the Elderly and the Disabled

If you are responsible for children, the elderly, or disabled persons, you will want to take some extra precautions. These people are most likely to become frightened or endangered during a quake, and least able to help themselves. They often do not understand catastrophic events and are easily confused.

Children need frequent reminders of emergency procedures. Go through various scenarios with them, and have them talk their way through the actions they would take

Garden decoration frequently is overlooked when residences are inspected for potential damage in future quakes. Block walls, statuary—even mailboxes, may require strengthening or replacement. F. M. Hanna photo.

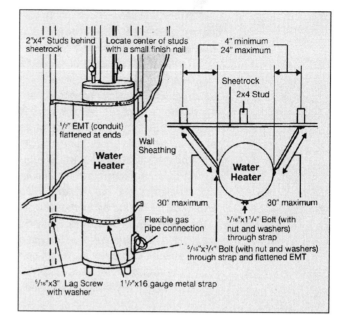

Strapping your home's water heater to the wall and making sure it is fitted with a flexible gas-supply line will greatly reduce the danger of fire or explosion from a gas leak after an earthquake. Diagram illustrates a typical tie-down, and indicates recommended materials. A licensed plumber may be needed to install the gas-supply line. Illustration courtesy of Bay Area Regional Earthquake Preparedness Project.

if you were not available to provide guidance and assistance. Expect them to feel afraid after a quake. Warn them about aftershocks.

If you are elderly or disabled, assess your own special needs and limitations. Know where to find help if you need it. If special equipment or medication is necessary to your well-being, keep it handy at all times. A small suitcase or bag should be accessible in case you have to scoop up these items and move them in a hurry.

Those with seeing-eye, handy companion or hearing dogs will need ready access to harness, equipment and pet food. Wheelchair-bound persons should know where to go in the house for maximum safety, and how to lock the wheels of the chair once they are in a safe and protected position. Bedridden patients need instruction on how to cover head and body with arms, pillows and blankets as protection from falling objects. A flashlight and whistle stored in a nightstand can be used to call for help or signal others if assistance is needed.

Enlarge your support area into the neighborhood, where the elderly may live alone. Tell them what to expect during and after a quake, and let them know whether you or someone else will be able to provide personal assistance or inspect their homes for them.

Personal Safety During an Earthquake

Most earthquakes hit and are over in less than 30 seconds, barely enough time to recognize that the motion you are feeling is an earthquake. A major catastrophic earthquake may produce shaking that lasts considerably longer.

If you have time to react, try to keep your senses even though everyone else around you is losing theirs:

1. Resist the temptation to do something, anything, to escape the quake. Even though it may be very difficult, do your best to stay calm. In almost all cases, the best procedure is to stay right where you are until the shaking stops.

2. If you are indoors, duck or drop down to the floor and take cover under a sturdy desk or table. Hold on to it and be prepared to move with it until the ground stops shaking. Move away from windows, fireplaces, wood stoves and heavy furniture or appliances. Stay inside; you may be injured going through a door or window, or be hit by falling glass, bricks, or unstable facades that may fall outward from buildings. If you are in a crowded area, stay calm and advise others on what to do. In a high-rise office building, stay where you are and wait for instructions from the building's emergency center; do not rush for elevators (they won't be operating) or stairwells (they probably will be jammed with panicky people).

3. If you are outside, stay there; move into the open, away from buildings and utility lines. If you are in a mountainous area, or near unstable slopes or cliffs, be alert for falling rocks or landslides. If you are at the beach, move to higher ground and find an escape route.

4. If you are walking in an area with multi-story commercial structures, particularly high-rise office buildings, move quickly into the middle of the street away from falling debris. Be alert for runaway vehicles.

All family members should know how to turn off utilities, if necessary, after a quake. The gas line is the most important utility, because a break could cause enough leakage to create a fire or explosion. A special wrench is usually needed to turn the valve. If there is danger from damaged electrical wires or overturned appliances, all electricity to the house can be shut down by turning off a single switch in the circuit-breaker or fuse box. Water can be turned off by closing either the valve in the meter box (a special tool may be required) or the gate valve on the main water line into the house. Illustration courtesy of Bay Area Regional Earthquake Preparedness Project.

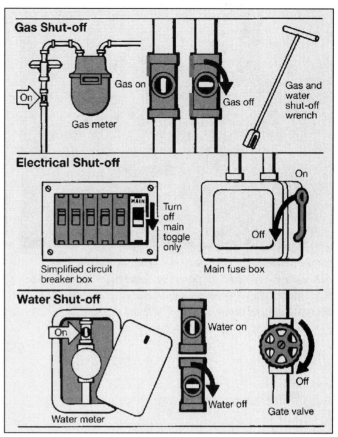

5. If you are driving, you may not even feel the earthquake because your vehicle's suspension system may soften or "soak up" the motions. If you are aware that an earthquake has started, move your car as far as possible out of the normal traffic pattern. Stop if it is safe; avoid stopping under overpasses, bridges, large trees, light posts, power lines or large signs. Stay inside your car until the shaking stops.

Checking For Damage After an Earthquake

A major earthquake can overwhelm local law enforcement, fire and emergency medical personnel and resources. You cannot expect these agencies to react immediately to problems at private homes—they will be busy attending to the needs of emergency centers and responding to crises in major business areas. If transportation and communication channels are damaged, finding help for your personal problems may take hours or days. Your best course of action is to assume personal responsibility for your own immediate area during the first crucial hours after the quake.

The first thing to do is check for personal injuries. Administer first aid if needed for minor problems; do not move seriously injured persons unless they are in immediate danger of further injuries.

As soon as possible, check for damage that could cause a fire, flood or other catastrophe. If it is dark, use a flashlight or battery-powered lantern. Do not smoke or use lighters and candles until you are sure there are no gas leaks. Shut off the main gas valve only if a leak is sus-

pected or identified by the odor of natural gas. Wait for the utility company to turn the gas back on. If electrical wiring is damaged, shut off power at the control box. Stay away from downed or damaged utility lines. If water lines are broken and there is danger of flooding, turn off the water supply at the main valve.

Inspect the building for fallen objects, and set them upright if you can do so easily. Be careful when you open closets and cupboards; displaced objects may fall when you open the door. Clean up any spills of medicines, combustible liquids, or other potentially harmful materials. If the building has a chimney, inspect it from a distance for damage. A strong aftershock can topple a chimney already weakened by an earlier quake.

Use the telephone or vehicles only in the event of life-threatening emergencies. Make sure all telephones are on their receivers; those off the hook tie up the telephone network unnecessarily.

During all of this, expect aftershocks. Most will be smaller than the main shake, but a few may be large enough to do additional damage to weakened structures. You may have to inspect the area a second time.

The time required to repair large-scale utility damage varies. Because major electrical systems can be restored by switching and redirecting power supplies, the lights can come back on surprisingly soon. After the 1994 Northridge earthquake, 93% of the area that suffered blackouts had electricity restored within 24 hours. Damaged gas, water and sewer lines often require more time for repair. Leaks and breaks have to be identified, the

Hillside homes require special attention and in most cases, specific anti-earthquake designs. Both the slope and the stability of the soils are important, because of landslide dangers within fault zones. Differential settling of the structure can occur if part is built on solid rock, and part on unconsolidated material. Photo by F. M. Hanna.

Immediately after a quake, all interior rooms should be inspected for damage or potential danger to occupants. Light fixture ring could be shaken down by an aftershock. Spillage from cabinets could have been prevented had safety latches been installed before the quake.

affected piece of the system has to be blocked off, labor-intensive and time-consuming repairs have to be made, and the new linkups must be tested before service can be restored. This can result in delays of 3-5 days.

Earthquake News

After a major earthquake, there will be no shortage of news reports on radio and television. Watch and listen, and use the information to help you decide the best course of action during the confusion that typifies the first 24 hours after the quake.

Rely on official announcements from reliable government agencies. Don't expect immediate, complete information. Mass media, in a frantic rush to beat each other on earthquake coverage, may exaggerate damage by passing along non-confirmed information and "eye-witness accounts" from untrained observers. Because few people know much about the origin and motion of earthquakes, anyone who can link the terms "magnitude," "San Andreas fault" and "collapse" in the same sentence may be considered an expert. Do not pay attention to rumors, and do not spread them.

If electricity and phone service are available, home computers can be valuable in disseminating information via electronic mail and bulletin boards, if the news is valid. Ham radio operators also play a critical role in relaying information.

If a house or office must be evacuated because of structural weakness or utility damage, make an effort to post some sort of handwritten sign in front to alert police and firefighters to the danger.

Recovery

While it's going on, a major earthquake can cause panic. When it's over, the resulting damage can cause major mental depression that is hard to relieve except by accepting the situation and starting over. Try to clean up the mess. Start making repairs to your home as soon as practical--both to restore your lifestyle, and to rid yourself of the sense of personal loss.

Earthquake damage to buildings often goes beyond the obvious. Studies after the 1994 Northridge quake determined that hundreds of buildings in West Los Angeles and the San Fernando Valley suffered hidden structural damage--primarily damage on welds and joints between columns and beams--that could undermine their resistance to a future quake. There are no laws requiring owners to reinforce these buildings, or to inform occupants of the added risk. Only individual responsibility will prompt the necessary inspections and often expensive repairs after a major quake.

Quality reconstruction work is critical. Property owners who do not fully repair their buildings after a major earthquake are setting the stage for substantial and sometimes surprising damage the next time a weak quake strikes the same spot. "Paint and plaster" can cover weakened joints and sagging frames; however, the building remains vulnerable to collapse unexpectedly months or even years later when subjected to another quake.

Even chimneys that are damaged but remain standing after a major quake may turn out to be a problem later, if a strong aftershock generates just enough new shock waves to complete the collapse. Diagram illustrates how to minimize chimney damage by strapping lower sections to the house and replacing upper part with a metal flue. Diagram courtesy of California Seismic Safety Commission Homeowner's Guide to Earthquake Safety.

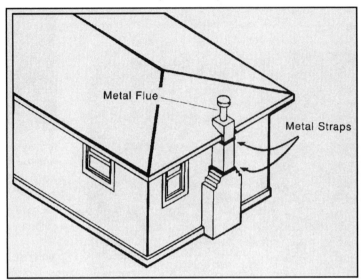

Several days were required to dig out all of the victims of the Veterans Hospital collapse after the 1971 earthquake. In general, emergency procedures after the quake worked very well. Los Angeles Times photo.

Fewer deaths result from California earthquakes than fatalities from shakes in other parts of the world, primarily because of our high construction standards. Loss of life has been minimal even when buildings collapsed.

CALIFORNIA QUAKES RESULTING IN MORE THAN 10 DEATHS

This is the surprisingly short list of California earthquakes that resulted in 10 or more deaths. Totals include those deaths attributed to heart attacks, which sometimes elevates the number significantly. Of 60 deaths in the 1994 Northridge quake, only 35 were the direct result of the earthquake.

Fatality estimates for 19th Century quakes—and even for 1906—are nothing more than estimates, because accurate records were not available. The total of 60 deaths for the 1872 quake, in particular, is suspect and may have been considerably less.

These totals are extremely low when compared to loss of life in earthquakes in other parts of the world, where thousands of people are killed every year. About 15,000 died in one quake in Iran in 1981, 5,000 in Algeria in 1980, and more than 3,000 in a 1980 quake in Italy. Five quakes in 1976—in China, Guatemala, New Guinea, Turkey, and the Philippines—accounted for about 300,000 deaths in that single year. Almost 2,000 deaths were recorded in the M7.5 quake that hit the remote Russian city of Neftegorsk at 1 a.m. on May 28, 1995.

There are many reasons for the inordinately high totals elsewhere. Of the reasons for the lower numbers in California, one of the most significant is the high quality of design and construction built into most modern California structures. Despite some singular and highly publicized exceptions, death tolls remain low even when there is significant property loss. Fortunately, several of the state's potentially disastrous quakes occurred when office buildings and schools were unoccupied.

Forecasts of fatalities from future California quakes of M7.0 or higher during daylight hours in highly populated areas exceed 1,000.

Date	Location	Deaths
April 18, 1906	San Francisco	Originally reported as 600, but probably closer to 3,000 over the entire affected area
March 11, 1933	Long Beach	115
February 9, 1971	San Fernando	65
October 18, 1989	Loma Prieta	62
January 17, 1994	Northridge	60
March 26, 1872	Owens Valley	60
December 8, 1812	San Juan Capistrano	40
October 21, 1868	Hayward	30
June 29, 1925	Santa Barbara	13
July 21, 1952	Kern County	12

A VISUAL INVENTORY

To document damage to your home and loss of personal possessions from an earthquake, fire or any other disaster, it's a good idea to make a detailed visual inventory of your furniture and possessions, including vehicles.

Color photographs or a videotape are best. Include appliances, antiques and other valuable items in all parts of the house, garage, basement and attic. Open closet and cupboard doors so small items on shelves are visible to the camera. Walk around the property and photograph garden walls, sheds, or any other structures that might be damaged.

Collect receipts for major purchases of art and antiques and make a list of prices and dates of purchase. Record serial numbers of computers, television sets, appliances and other major electrical items.

Label and date the photos or videotape, and any lists or receipts. Store all of this in a safe-deposit box; do not keep it in the house where it might be lost during an earthquake or fire.

State regulations regarding earthquake insurance change annually, as the legislature attempts to work out a program that will satisfy both consumers and the insurance companies. The company that insures your home for fire probably will be able to provide earthquake insurance. But the extent of the coverage and exclusions are subject to change. To find out the current status, contact your insurance agent or call the California State Department of Insurance at 800-927-4357.

Sources of Information

EARTHQUAKE INFORMATION TELEPHONE HOTLINES:

USGS, Menlo Park: 415-329-4025

University of California Seismographic Station: 510-642-2160

Cal Tech, Pasadena: 818-395-6977

Humboldt State Earthquake Education Center, Arcata: 707-826-6020

National Earthquake Information Center, Golden CO: 303-273-8516

EARTHQUAKE INFORMATION WORLD WIDE WEB SITES:

Southern California Earthquake Center:
http://www.usc.edu/dept/earth/quake/

U. S. Geological Survey:
http://www.usgs.gov/

National Earthquake Information Center:
http://www.usgs.gov/data/geologic/neic/index.html

California Division of Mines and Geology:
http://www.consrv.ca.gov/

GOVERNMENT AGENCIES:

The U.S. Geological Survey Earth Science Information Center answers questions from scientists and the general public, and provides maps and publications about the state's seismicity:

345 Middlefield Road
Menlo Park, CA 94025
415-329-4390

**Recent Earthquake Activity:
USGS office in Menlo Park**
http://quake.usgs.gov/

The National Earthquake Information Center of the U.S. Geological Survey reports on all aspects of earthquake activity throughout the world; Earthquakes And Volcanoes is a bimonthly publication for laymen.

Box 25046
Denver Federal Center, MS 967
Denver, CO 80225
303-273-8500

The National Geophysical Data Center has publications on the Earth's structure and atmosphere.

325 Broadway
Boulder, CO 80303
303-497-6215

The California Division of Mines and Geology maintains three offices. Many publications on faults and earthquakes are available for small fees; California Geology is a monthly publication for laymen.

801 K Street, 14th Floor
Sacramento, CA 95812-2980
916-445-5716

California Division of Mines and Geology:
185 Berry Street
San Francisco, CA 94107-1728
415-904-7707

107 South Broadway, Room #1065
Los Angeles, CA 90012
213-620-3560

The Humboldt Earthquake Education Center answers questions about the north coast area; its popular educational booklet is entitled On Shaky Ground—Living with Earthquakes on the North Coast.

Humboldt State University
Arcata, CA 95521-8299
707-826-3931

The following three regional offices focus on the study of earthquakes and provide literature, videotapes and slide shows on preparedness:

Bay Area Regional Earthquake Preparedness Project
101 8th Street, Suite 152
Oakland CA 94607
510-893-0818

Southern California Earthquake Preparedness Project
1110 East Green St., Suite 300
Pasadena, CA 91106
818-795-9055

Southern California Earthquake Preparedness Project
1350 Front St., Suite 4015
San Diego, CA 92101
619-525-4287

Federal Emergency Management Agency (FEMA) maintains two California offices:

The Presidio, Building 105
San Francisco, CA 94129
415-923-7100
245 South Los Robles
Pasadena, CA 91101
818-451-3000

The California Seismic Safety Commission has publications on construction guidelines for earthquake zones, hazard reduction in buildings and emergency planning.

1900 K Street, Suite 100

Sacramento, CA 95814-4186
916-322-4917

The American Red Cross has two main offices in California; they can provide multi-lingual handbooks and audiovisual materials on earthquake and disaster preparedness.

2700 Wilshire Blvd
Los Angeles, CA 90057
213-739-5200

1550 Sutter St
San Francisco, CA 94109
415-202-0780

The California Office of Emergency Services has two offices; its publications include two about Living On The Fault, focusing on the San Andreas and Hayward fault zones.

2800 Meadowview Rd.
Sacramento, CA 95832
916-262-1843
1110 E. Green Street, Ste. 300
Pasadena, CA 91106
818-304-8383

If you need help in locating professional engineers and contractors:

Contractors State License Board
P.O. Box 26000
Sacramento, CA 95826
916-255-3900

For technical publications, videotapes, slide sets, and other reports on earthquakes around the world, of special interest to urban and regional planners:

Earthquake Engineering Research Institute
499 14th Street, Suite 320
Oakland, CA 94612-1934
510-451-0905

For the latest information on reducing seismic risks in earthquake-prone metropolitan areas, including maps and publications on ground-shaking probabilities:

Association of Bay Area Governments
101 8th Street
P.O. Box 2050
Oakland, CA
510-464-7900

Southern California Association of Governments
818 W. 7th St., 12th Floor
Los Angeles, CA 90017
213-236-1800

San Diego Association of Governments
401 B St., Ste. 800
San Diego, CA 92101
619-595-5300

WHERE WERE YOU WHEN THE EARTHQUAKE HIT?

The staff of the Department of Geology at Humboldt State University is part of a scientific team studying the effects of recent and historic earthquakes on the West Coast. You can help us by filling out this questionnaire about your personal experiences in any large quake that strikes your area. Although scientists can accurately determine the location of the earthquake and its magnitude from sophisticated instruments, we cannot quantify the earthquake's effects on people without the input of people who felt the earthquake. Information taken from these questionnaires can be used to improve emergency planning for future earthquakes.

Please answer as many questions as you can; incomplete responses are better than no responses at all. Please include your location during the earthquake. We don't need a specific address, but give as much information as you can-- town name, closest major intersections, distance from city hall or other prominent buildings. The information you provide is completely confidential; it is not necessary to include your name and address, unless you choose to do so.

If you have any questions, please contact the Humboldt Earthquake Education Center, 707-826-6019. Mail the completed questionnaire to:

Department of Geology
Humboldt State University
Arcata, CA 95521

Questionnaire

1. Location/Address: Where were you during the earthquake (Give address or location) as precisely as possible.

_____

2. Situation: What was your situation during the earthquake?
a. Were you (circle):

INSIDE   OUTSIDE   DRIVING (speed.......................)

b. If inside, type of building (circle):

SINGLE-FAMILY HOME/DUPLEX
APARTMENT BLDG. (FLOOR ....)   MOBILEHOME

OTHER:_____

_____

3. What was your position when you felt the earthquake:

LYING DOWN   SITTING   STANDING   WALKING

OTHER:_____

If you were asleep, did the earthquake wake you up?

NO   YES

_____

4. Your experience of the earthquake:
a. How would you describe the ground shaking:

WEAK   MILD   MODERATE   STRONG   VIOLENT

b. How did you react?

VERY LITTLE REACTION   EXCITEMENT
SOMEWHAT FRIGHTENED   VERY FRIGHTENED
PANIC

c. Was it difficult to stand or walk?

NO   YES

_____

5. Earthquake effects:
a. Did objects topple over or fall off shelves?

NO   JUST A FEW   MANY   EVERYTHING

b. Did pictures on walls move or get knocked askew?

NO   YES   DIDN'T NOTICE

c. Did any furniture or appliances slide, tip over, or become displaced?

NO   YES

d. Was there any damage to the building?

NO   YES   NOT SURE

(If yes, please describe damage, such as cracks in walls, ceilings, or floors; broken windows; broken pipe lines; water heater pulled away from wall; damage to chimney or foundation; collapse of wall, ceiling or porches; etc.).

e. Did you notice any dust in the air during or after the earthquake?

NO   YES   DIDN'T NOTICE

If yes, please describe:

_____

6. Do you have any additional comments or observations about the earthquake (use a separate page if necessary)?

Index

Entries in boldface indicate illustrations; italics indicate years of major earthquakes.